RAVENNA   FEB 1 2002

WITHDRAWN

021074

JB
Ward   Furbee, Mary R.
             Wild rose : Nancy Ward and the Cherokee
          Nation / Mary R. Furbee. -- Morgan
          Reynolds, c2002.

MUSKEGON COUNTY LIBRARY

    I. Title.

WILD ROSE
Nancy Ward and the Cherokee Nation

WILD ROSE
Nancy Ward and the Cherokee Nation

Mary R. Furbee

MORGAN
REYNOLDS
Publishers, Inc.
620 South Elm Street, Suite 223
Greensboro, North Carolina 27406
http://www.morganreynolds.com

WILD ROSE: NANCY WARD AND THE CHEROKEE NATION

Copyright © 2002 by Mary R. Furbee

All rights reserved.
This book, or parts thereof, may not be reproduced in any form except by written consent of the publisher. For information write:
Morgan Reynolds, Inc., 620 S. Elm St., Suite 223
Greensboro, North Carolina 27406 USA

Cover image © Stock Montage

Library of Congress Cataloging-in-Publication Data

Furbee, Mary R. (Mary Rodd), 1954-
 Wild Rose : Nancy Ward and the Cherokee Nation / Mary R. Furbee.
   p. cm.
 Includes bibliographical references and index.
 ISBN 1-883846-71-4 (lib. bgd. : alk. paper)
  1. Ward, Nancy, d. 1822--Juvenile literature. 2. Cherokee women--Biography--Juvenile literature. 3. Cherokee Indians--Kings and rulers--Biography--Juvenile literature. [1. Ward, Nancy, d. 1822. 2. Cherokee Indians--Biography. 3. Indians of North America--Biography. 4. Women--Biography.] I. Title.

E99.C5 W264 2001
975'.0049755'0092--dc21
[B]
                                                              00-054884

Printed in the United States of America
First Edition

For my WVU School of Journalism students,
who inspire me everyday

The author wishes to thank the Appalachian Life Foundation of Morgantown, West Virginia, for a grant to help with research during the writing of this book.

Contents

Chapter One
  Green Corn Festival 9
Chapter Two
  Early Losses 27
Chapter Three
  Beloved Woman 42
Chapter Four
  Respite 60
Chapter Five
  Division 67
Chapter Six
  Long Island Treaty 78
Chapter Seven
  Concessions 88
Chapter Eight
  Granny Ward 96
Afterword
  The Trail of Tears 103

Bibliography 105
Index 110

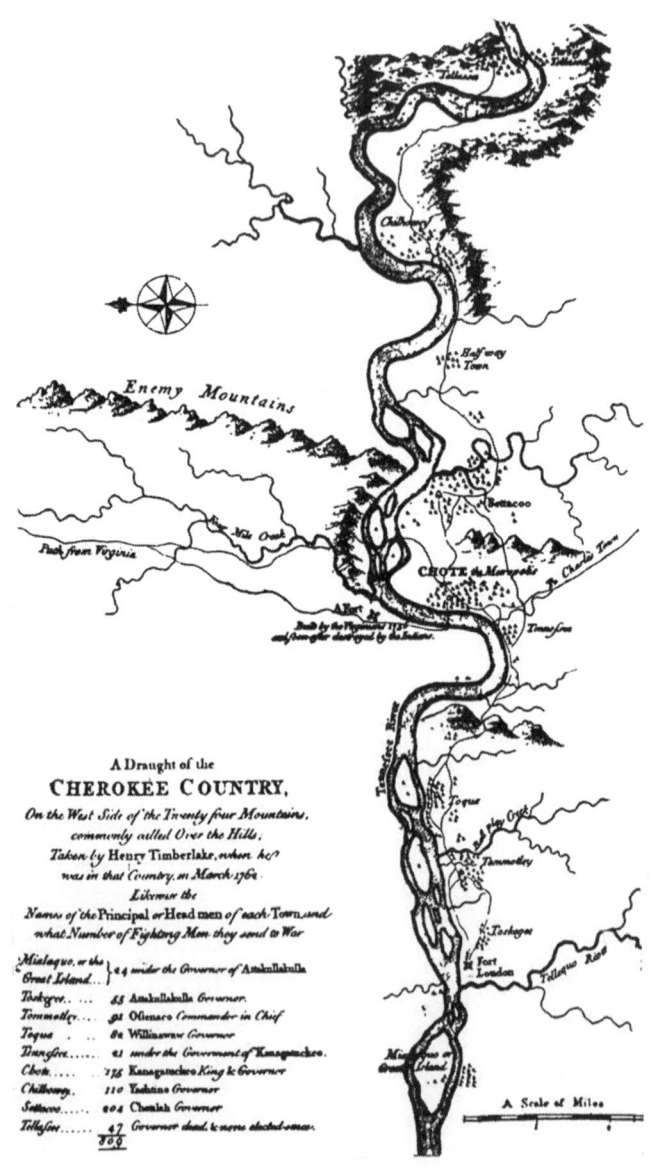

The land of the Cherokee Nation at the time of Nancy Ward.

Chapter One

Green Corn Festival

As the rosy light of a new day filtered through the smoke hole of her family's house, eight-year-old Nanye-hi awoke. In the center of the oblong room, Nanye-hi's mother, Tame Doe, squatted by the household fire. For a solid year, that fire had never gone out. Now Tame Doe muttered a prayer under her breath as she smothered the glowing embers with white sand from the Little Tennessee River.

Nanye-hi waited until her mother turned away from the fire before she scrambled out from under her fawn-skin blanket, pulled on her skirt, and trotted to the door. She pulled open the heavy plank door and peered out into the town square of Chota. It was no ordinary day in the Land of the Blue Smoke. Nanye-hi could hardly wait for it to begin.

Tame Doe called, "Wild Rose!" and Nanye-hi scur-

Nancy Ward

ried back to help her mother. Nanye-hi's nickname came from the fragrant woodland rose, for at birth her cheeks flushed a deep pink. Nanye-hi and her mother had a busy day ahead. Nanye-hi's brother, Long Fellow, had left before dawn. Through a fog of sleep, Nanye-hi had seen him pad as soft-footed as a wildcat across the single room. He grabbed a leftover corn cake from last night's supper and crept silently outside. Like Nanye-hi, he too was eager to start this day.

Nanye-hi was not bothered that her brother had left before dawn. Their mother would only have made him feed their wolf pups before letting him go play ball with his cousins and friends. It was Nanye-hi who helped her mother in the house and fields, not Long Fellow.

Nanye-hi could hear the *Ani-Yunwiya*, the Real People, already gathering outside. The priests had announced it was time for the Green Corn Festival. Messengers had spread the word among the sixty-five Cherokee towns in the Appalachian Mountains south of the wide Ohio River. About 12,000 Cherokee lived along the Tennessee, Kanawha, and Savannah rivers and tributaries. The Cherokee Nation's capital, Chota, was in present-day Monroe County, Tennessee. Every summer Chota hosted the Green Corn Festival. A week

The Cherokee Nation

Nanye-hi took her nickname from the wild rose.

of trading, feasting, games, dancing, and singing marked the beginning of a new year. The chiefs of the sixty self-governing towns would also hold a tribal council to discuss events and concerns of all the Real People. By the white settlers' calendar, the year was 1745.

The early morning mist rose off the river as Nanye-hi and Tame Doe prepared their home for the coming year. During the past weeks, they had repainted the inside and outside walls of the house with white clay and placed fresh rushes on the roof. Now they swept the packed dirt floor, placed new bedding on the raised couches, and threw away worn-out clothing. Afterwards, Nanye-hi and her mother left their house to help gather the seven sacred woods.

With a laughing group of Chota's women and children, Nanye-hi and her mother entered the forest to collect the seven sacred woods: white oak, black

 **Nancy Ward**

oak, water oak, blackjack, basswood, chestnut, and white pine. They stripped branches, twigs, and inner bark from dead trees on the forest floor and hauled them back to town in giant baskets that they strapped to their foreheads.

The Chota firemaker, who lived in the hilltop Council House and cared for the sacred fire, accepted the wood. Tassels of fawn fur swung about the firemaker's scarf as he solemnly set about renewing the *Atsila Galunkweti Yu*, or sacred fire, that burned always. As he worked, the firemaker sang a song from when the world was young.

The firemaker's song told how an evil conjurer stole the People's fire and turned it into small white crystals that told the future. The People sent a young Cherokee boy to recover the fire, who used magic to trick the conjurer. The boy asked the conjurer to let him see the future in the stones. The conjurer agreed and held out the stones. As he did, a flame rose out of the crystals. The young boy threw tobacco on the fire, causing the flames to jump, and the evil conjurer was burned alive. Since then, evil has been imprisoned in the fire. As long as the sacred fire burned, the Cherokee would survive.

The refreshed sacred fire flared, then died down as

The Cherokee Nation

the firemaker sang. With a forked stick, the firemaker raked out a pile of glowing embers and gave a few to each Chota woman. Tame Doe cradled her embers in a seashell as she and Nanye-hi walked home. As their ancestors had since the beginning of time, they built a new fire inside their circle of stones. With fire, the connection between heaven and earth was renewed.

Nanye-hi finished helping Tame Doe in the house, and then she ran to the kennel. The family's litter of wolf pups yipped and howled when they saw her coming with scraps and bones from last night's meal. Nanye-hi laughed as the growling pups dived on the scraps she threw over the fence. At last, Nanye-hi was finished with work and ready to join the festival.

In the central square, Nanye-hi scampered about looking at the trade goods the seven Cherokee clans had brought. Nanye-hi fingered the Bird Clan's snares and blowguns and the Paint Clan's love potions. An especially colorful pile of wampum caught her eye, too. The Real People valued the pretty shell, clay, and glass beads as much as the English did silver and gold, especially the milky strands of river mussel pearls.

Nanye-hi nudged her way through a large crowd in front of grizzled Old Weasel's lodge. The English trader had lived with the Cherokee since Tame Doe

 # Nancy Ward

was a young girl. Old Weasel bought beaver and deer furs from the Cherokee and sold them guns, powder, metal arrow points, glass bottles, iron kettles, and more. Once a year, the trader piled his furs onto a long wagon pulled by many horses. Then he followed the Great Trading Path through the Appalachian Mountains to Charles Town, South Carolina. There, Old Weasel sold his furs to rich white men that lived in houses made of red, baked stone. The Charles Town traders put the furs in giant canoes, sent them across the great water, and sold them to even richer men, the trader said.

Old Weasel's trading post often bustled with activity. But during the annual Green Corn Festival, it was jammed. Nanye-hi pushed her way to the front of the crowd. Men and women laden with deer and beaver hides waited patiently to trade for Old Weasel's goods. The men examined new rifles and West Indian tobacco. The women fingered Old Weasel's new shipment of cloth, petticoats, steel needles, ribbons, scissors, and looking glasses. Nanye-hi watched as a man paid thirty-five deer hides for a rifle and a woman traded fourteen hides for a white cotton petticoat.

Through the crowd, Nanye-hi caught sight of her young cousins from the Wolf Clan and ran to join them.

The Cherokee Nation

Laughing, the girls joined hands and swung in a circle. Chattering nonstop, they ran off to watch the rough-and-tumble game of *anetsa* that had begun at dawn. The rugged game, played with a stick and a ball, solved many disputes between different clans and towns. Many arms and legs got broken, too, so the medicine men kept a good supply of herbs, potions, and splints handy.

Nanye-hi and her cousins arrived at the field just as the ball was tossed into the air. Nanye-hi pointed out Long Fellow to her companions. One of Long Fellow's young teammates caught the ball with a net fastened on one end of a long stick, and the children cheered. He dropped the ball into his hand and ran toward the goal at the end of the field. Guards from the opposite team tackled his teammates, and down Long Fellow went. Nanye-hi laughed as the young men rolled about the grass like a nest of wrestling wildcats.

The Green Corn Festival was always exciting. But to members of the Wolf Clan—the largest and most important of the seven clans—this year's festival was doubly special. Tame Doe's brother, Attakullakulla, was to be named the peace chief of Chota. He would join the chiefs, priests, war captains, and honored women on the town council. Larger towns had a peace

 Nancy Ward

chief and a war chief who were a part of the council of elders. The title was an honor in all the People's self-governing towns. But Chota was the Nation's capital, so its peace and war chiefs were among the Nation's most influential leaders.

The Green Corn Festival began on the evening of the new moon. Nanye-hi crawled through the hollow log opening into the huge seven-sided Council House. Under a high roof held up by ten pillars, several hundred Cherokee feasted together on milky green corn roasted inside the husks and on a buck deer cooked on a spit over the new sacred fire.

After the meal, it was time for the *Anagahunshu*, or Green Corn Dance. The People danced for hours. Gray-haired elders pounded a great stone drum shaped like a turtle. Others played water drums and gourd rattles. A full belly and the hypnotic drumming made Nanye-hi's eyelids heavy, but she shook herself wide awake so she would miss nothing. The dancers' bare feet beating the ground sounded like startled pheasants flying out of tangled laurel thickets. The circles advanced and retreated, forward and back, around and around. The drummers and singers called their song, and the dancers responded in a chorus.

The dances continued through the night. Men and

The Cherokee Nation

A typical eighteenth-century Cherokee man.

women, young and old, took turns circling, twirling, stomping, advancing, and retreating. The men's shaved heads glistened with bear grease. From the single patch of hair on the backside of each man's head dangled silver pendants, deer fur, beads, or feathers. Copper and silver wire glittered in their stretched ear lobes, and animal, star, and moon tattoos adorned their chests and arms. But Nanye-hi especially loved to watch the women dancers. Their fine, soft deerskin skirts and cloaks decorated with peacock feathers and shells were beautiful. When Tame Doe danced, red and white ribbons swirled about her single long braid and her narrow feet stepped lightly on the earth. The fire flickered and cracked and smoke billowed overhead. Nanye-hi fell asleep that night against her mother's shoulder.

The next morning, Tame Doe shook Nanye-hi awake, and with the rest of the People they circled the Council House. A priest sprinkled the dressed skin of the buck deer with fresh blood from a bird, and everyone walked down to the river. Facing east, the People plunged in the cold water seven times to cleanse themselves of evil thoughts and deeds.

The Chota chiefs, Oconostota and Attakullakulla, left the water first, followed by other chiefs and all the

The Cherokee Nation

People. They walked to the summer pavilion painted with white clay, touched a crystal the priest held, and took a piece of medicinal root from a pile.

When all had passed, the priest spoke a prophecy. He said that the Real People had a great task ahead of them. A white ball from east would come and the People's grandchildren would go west. Then they would have great trials and be divided into different factions. Families would divide against each other, and many would disregard their chiefs, leaders, medicine men, and captains. But if the younger generation followed the Great Spirit's instruction, there would be a chance to turn back east.

The People fasted for days after purifying themselves in the river. Then the Nation assembled under the Council House's thatched roof again. Nanye-hi and her mother sat with other Wolf Clan members on benches lined with hemp rugs. A priest cast old tobacco and a buck's tongue on the fire. Then the People broke their fast with venison and cornmeal mush sweetened with mulberries from their groves. Around Nanye-hi, several hundred men, women, and children gathered to honor her favorite uncle, Attakullakulla, the new Chota Peace Chief.

The Raven, a great warrior, rose to speak first. The

Nancy Ward

winds from the east had brought victory in war to the Cherokee, he said, his voice carrying to every corner. The great Chota war chief, Oconostota, had heard the wind and led the People in war. But Chota had for too long been without a chief to hear the south wind's gentle message of peace. Attakullakulla would hear and speak these messages to the People. He would oversee the everyday affairs of the capital, meet with visitors from foreign nations, and coordinate annual festivals. Attakullakulla's wisdom would help him guide the Real People down the white path of peace.

Nanye-hi listened proudly to the Raven's words and the many speeches that followed. Many *Unakas*, or white people like Old Weasel, used lines on paper to remember their words, but the Real People spoke of the past, present, and future from their hearts. The words were often repeated and never forgotten.

The fire cast dancing shadows on the whitewashed walls as another priest rose. He spoke of how Cherokee children had once inherited titles such as chief, priest, and conjurer from their parents. But the corrupt *Kootenai*, or ancient priests, had abused their power. The Kootenai grew so arrogant that they kidnapped other men's wives. So, the Cherokee banded together and executed the priests. After that, the People's titles were earned, not passed down from father to son or mother to daughter. The Chota Council had deemed Attakullakulla worthy to become peace chief, the priest finished, for he respected the laws of harmony, did not fear strangers, and was devoted to the white road of peace.

Nanye-hi knew the priest spoke the truth, for she was closer to her uncle Attakullakulla than her own father, Five Killer. Tame Doe had married Five Killer, a Lenne Lenapi warrior. But not long after Nanye-hi was born, Five Killer and Tame Doe "split the blanket." While most Cherokee marriages lasted a long time, this was not always so. If the couple did not wish to remain married, either partner could end the union. The split did not affect Nanye-hi greatly, for it was the People's custom that maternal uncles raised the children of their sisters. Therefore, Nanye-hi's closest relatives were her mother's brothers, members of the Wolf Clan. Nanye-hi was especially close to Attakullakulla.

At eight years old, Nanye-hi stood nearly five feet tall—almost shoulder to shoulder with her tiny Uncle Attakullakulla. Her uncle's slight frame had not lessened him in the People's eyes. A man's words and deeds, not his size, bought him honor. From boyhood,

Nancy Ward

Attakullakulla had won many friends with his charming smile, kind heart, and persuasive talk. Attakullakulla never forgot a face and always returned favors. His friends said affectionately that Attakullakulla could talk an eagle out of its tail.

Attakullakulla took his place on the Chota Council. Nanye-hi glanced over at his three sons, Dragging Canoe, Badger, and Little Owl, who sat with her brother, Long Fellow. The teenage boys could not hide their excitement as the Chota war chief, Oconostota, held up a mantle of swan feathers. Seven red and black stripes crisscrossed the war chief's face, and a long red stripe stretched from his forehead to his chest. Oconostota draped the cloak across Attakullakulla's wiry shoulders, and the new peace chief's elf-like face shone with joy. The priests, war captains, conjurers, healers, and honored men and women of the Chota Council cheered with the rest of the People.

When the Council House quieted, Chief Oconostota spoke of the People's past. The Real People had once lived alone in the mountainous Land of the Blue Smoke, Oconostota said. But in his grandfather's time, white men came from the east to trade with the Cherokee. Some of the traders had proven to be true friends. But others cheated the People and sold Chero-

The Cherokee Nation

kee children as slaves. Some of the People moved south and west, hoping to escape the whites. But the English kept coming, and the People waged war to get their children back. Some towns grew angry with the English and began trading instead with the French, who had lodges along the Mississippi.

Then an Englishman named Alexander Cuming came to visit the Cherokee, and the path was made clean. Cuming made a beautiful speech. Fire burned in his deep-set eyes, and brave talk streamed from his wide mouth. The barrel of his musket gleamed, as did the brass buttons on his long, red coat. Cuming said that the English king considered the Cherokee his beloved children. King George II, Cuming said, would punish any British subjects who cheated or enslaved the Cherokee. The King wanted to keep the trading path clean between their two nations. To prove this, he invited representatives of the tribe to visit his Council House across the big water.

Nanye-hi knew that Oconostota was leading up to Attakullakulla's visit to London. Nanye-hi had begged her uncle many times to tell her of the great journey he took several years before her birth. Attakullakulla and six other young warriors had accepted Cuming's invitation. They crossed the ocean with fish as big as

 Nancy Ward

horses and waves as tall as the forest in a great canoe pushed by the wind. Cuming called his great ship the *Fox*.

Attakullakulla had seen marvelous things in England. In the town of London, people rode in small houses on wheels pulled by horses draped in silver and gold. The women's clothes were as colorful as the brightest birds' feathers, and their big hair—curled and piled on top of their heads—looked like squirrels' nests. Attakullakulla had been most impressed by King George's stone Council House. It was as big as the entire town of Chota and had many doors. A river surrounded it, and a great gate fell across the river to become a bridge.

Attakullakulla had visited King George II in his throne room and kissed the king's baby-soft hand. Many rings twinkled like colored stars on King George's fat fingers. The Cherokee delegation presented the king with a crown of possum fur dyed red and decorated with scalps and eagle tails. They gave a mulberry bark carpet made by the women of Chota to Queen Anne. By the end of the visit, Attakullakulla and the others had sworn undying allegiance to the rich and powerful English King. They also signed a paper promising to trade only with the British. "Although

The Cherokee Nation

you are white and we are red, our hands and hearts are joined together," a warrior called Prince told the king. "The great King's enemies shall be our enemies. His people and ours shall be as one, and we shall die together."

The King thanked the Cherokee men for the gifts and oath of loyalty. In return, he gave them a giant canoe loaded with more guns, ammunition, red paint, and glass beads than they had ever seen before. The warriors took their gifts back across the river. The peace between England and the Cherokee Nation had lasted for fifteen years.

Oconostota paused, and his voice became a low, sad rumble. Soon after Attakullakulla's return from England, he said, a great sorrow had afflicted the People. The black spirit of death had arrived on the west wind, killing many and scarring more. White traders said the disease, called "small pox," came from African slave ships. The medicine men said evil spirits had sent the disease, and they danced the Booger Dance to drive them away. The medicine men also gave the sick steam baths in the People's hothouses and then plunged them into the cold river.

But the medicine men had lost their power, Oconostota explained, and half the People died.

 Nancy Ward

Attakullakulla also caught the sickness, and the pox left his face covered with pitted scars. The People valued beauty so much that some maimed men and women could not stand the grief and threw themselves into the sacred fire. But Attakullakulla had been strong and survived so that he might now serve his people.

Chapter Two

Early Losses

Nanye-hi grew more like a woman with every passing moon. Tame Doe showed her how to concoct a potion from the sumac bush that made her hair as soft as woodland moss and as sleek as river water. Young warriors began to cast quick glances at Nanye-hi's knee-length raven-black hair, clear skin, and wide eyes. She was thirteen-years-old, old enough to marry. But Nanye-hi was not ready. She still had much to learn and experience on her own.

Nanye-hi was born in 1737, the year small pox disfigured her uncle and killed half the Cherokee. Although many infants and young children died, Nanye-hi had thrived. Tame Doe said her daughter was protected by the *Nunne'hi*, the invisible and immortal spirit people who lived under the hills. The name *Nanye-hi* meant "she who walks with the spirit people."

 Nancy Ward

Nanye-hi believed she was protected by the Nunne'hi, too. At night she curled up under her soft blanket and listened to the wind rustling through the forest. She heard twigs crack as panthers stalked their prey and the gentle humming sound deer made as they scratched their backs on tree bark. She heard the whippoorwill's song of longing and the redheaded woodpecker gaily tapping out its tune. Sometimes, if she could stay awake long enough, Nanye-hi also heard the Nunne'hi singing to the stars.

The spirit people enchanted beautiful women and handsome young men who heard the enticing song, Attakullakulla said. The spellbound young people slipped from their beds and followed the song into the forest and never returned. But Nanye-hi never left her bed to follow the Nunne'hi. If ever she was lost in the woods, Nanye-hi was certain the Nunne'hi would not steal her away. Instead, they would take her by the hand and bring her safely home.

Like Tame Doe, the honored women of the tribal council saw something special in Nanye-hi. As she grew, the honored women joined Attakullakulla in teaching her ancient tales, rituals, and ways. She learned how the Cherokee first got fire and why men hunted the forest and ate their animal brothers and

The Cherokee Nation

sisters. She knew that, in the beginning, the earth had been flat, soft, and wet. Then a great-grandfather buzzard whose wings spread so wide that they shadowed the sun flew over the muddy land. Finally, weary from his flight, the great buzzard drooped its wings low. The wings scooped miles of soft dirt into great mountains and left behind deep valleys.

Nanye-hi also knew all the stories about Kanati and Selu, the patrons of male hunters and female farmers. She could name all seven sacred heavens, clans, ceremonies, trees, and directions. She knew the Real People lived in the center of the universe, heavenly bodies lived in the skies above, and evil spirits lived below the earth. Yet Nanye-hi did not only learn of the past. The honored women looked after the People's well-being in the present, too. They discussed issues that affected Chota and the entire tribe. Chota, near present-day Knoxville, Tennessee, was one of the Overhill towns clustered along the Little Tennessee and Tellico rivers. The Cherokee's middle towns were in present-day southwest North Carolina. The lower towns were in present-day South Carolina and Georgia.

All the Cherokee towns had white traders. But as Nanye-hi grew older, many more came to live in the

 Nancy Ward

Overhill towns. Sickness had killed a great number of Cherokee men, so many widowed and single Cherokee women found husbands among the white traders. Enough of Nanye-hi's friends and cousins were of mixed blood that others sometimes called the Overhill Cherokee "the white Indians."

The Cherokee adopted the white husbands into the tribe and loved them. Many of the men loved the People in return and were fair traders. They brought horses, guns, tools, peach trees, coffee, and other fine goods that provided comfort and joy. But some traders turned out to be dishonest and greedy. Although it was against colonial laws to carry more than a few bottles of liquor into Cherokee country, some bad traders brought in many kegs of *amo-atsila*, or firewater. After "liquoring up" the Cherokee, the bad traders cheated them. The honored women often discussed this problem and counseled the People against drinking the white people's rum and whiskey.

Nanye-hi agreed that firewater was like poison to most Cherokee. A dipper of it stole their good sense. But Nanye-hi saw that this was true for some white people, too. Nanye-hi judged the white traders as she did her own People. Some were good, some were bad, and some were a mixture of both. Yet most brought

The Cherokee Nation

very useful tools to the Cherokee. The white man's muskets, rifles, and animal traps worked far better than the arrows and blowguns used by the People's grandfathers. The steel knives and iron tomahawks also cut much cleaner than stone ones. Nanye-hi still dug clay from along the creek banks to make pots, wove baskets from white oak, and did many things just as her grandmothers had. But not for anything would she and Tame Doe have given up the unbreakable iron pots that heated so evenly, or the steel needles that replaced the fragile bone ones.

Nanye-hi's family and many Overhill Cherokee were quick to adopt the white people's style of housing, too. Attakullakulla so loved the log houses of white traders and settlers that he asked white men to teach him how to build them. He then built himself a log house with a stone chimney and small, high windows for shooting through if under attack. Nanye-hi thought the stone chimney was a fabulous invention. The wind sucked smoke far better than the little hole in their stick and mud house. Attakullakulla helped Tame Doe and other Chota residents build log houses, too. The white traders, who had a hard time saying Attakullakulla, began calling the peace chief "Little Carpenter." They called Nanye-hi "Nancy."

 Nancy Ward

Nancy saw less of her uncle Little Carpenter after he became peace chief. Often he traveled to Winchester, Richmond, Charles Town, and other colonial cities to discuss trade and politics with the English rulers of the colonies. Too many colonists had been disobeying their King's commands and moving into the mountains. Unlike the traders, few of these whites married into the tribe and brought it wealth. Instead, the frontier settlers cut down the forests and sliced open the earth to plant crops. They also killed much of the game the Cherokee depended upon for meat and trade. Already, the elk, mountain lion, and red wolf were nearly gone.

Little Carpenter asked the British officials to stop these frontier colonists from coming across the mountains. The English tried, but land-hungry frontier families ignored them. Some of the middle and lower Cherokee towns that had weaker ties with the English grew fed up. Their warriors attacked the isolated frontier settlements established by trespassing whites, and the whites retaliated with equally bloody raids. Attakullakulla talked long and hard to convince the English that not all the Cherokee were on the warpath. But each time Nancy greeted her uncle on his return to Chota, the sparkle in his eyes seemed a bit dimmer.

At fifteen years old, Nancy had grown into a wil-

The Cherokee Nation

lowy and serious young woman with a thirst for learning and wisdom beyond her years. A handsome young man of the Deer Clan caught her eye, and she found less time for the honored women. Kingfisher's skin shined a coppery brown from rubbing it with the scarlet root that grew on low slopes. When he played stickball, his laugh carried far into the forest.

Once when Nanye-hi was telling stories to a group of small children, she looked up to see Kingfisher watching her with bright eyes. Kingfisher smiled, and Nancy's cheeks grew pink like a wild rose scorched by the sun. She met his eyes directly and smiled warmly in return. There was shyness in both their smiles, but courage, too. Nancy and Kingfisher began to spend time together, walking along the woodland trails, swimming in the river, and talking for hours. Soon the young couple knew that they never wanted to part.

Kingfisher told his mother that he and Nancy wanted to marry. Each was a member of a different clan and came from a respected family. Kingfisher's mother was pleased. She visited Tame Doe, and the two mothers agreed to the match. Seven days later, Nancy and Kingfisher stood together before the chiefs and honored ones. They wore red beads around their necks to ensure long life and success in love.

 Nancy Ward

Kingfisher faced Nancy and told her that his feet would walk on the paths before her. He gave Nancy a side of venison and promised to keep her supplied with meat. Nancy faced Kingfisher and said her feet would walk on the paths before him. She gave him an ear of corn and said she would grow food for him and their children in her fields. Nancy and Kingfisher held a white blanket and folded it together. Their two souls were joined as one.

During the next two years, Nancy gave birth to two children: a son, Five Killer, and a daughter, Ka-ti. Nancy and her children only saw Kingfisher during the moons of winter when the wild geese came to the People. In years past, Kingfisher and the other Chota men would have left for hunting trips that lasted only a few weeks. But now the tribe needed plenty of furs to trade for guns and ammunition, which they used to get more furs and to wage wars.

The competition for game and fur between the tribes fostered intertribal warfare. As the tribes pushed into new areas in their search, skirmishes over hunting rights erupted. Kingfisher fought against the Creek to the south, the Iroquois to the north, and the Shawnee to the west. Because the white men's guns were far deadlier than the arrows and blowguns of old, more

The Cherokee Nation

men were killed and wounded. Nancy gave Kingfisher special potions and stones for his medicine pouch. A warrior's death was an honorable one, but Kingfisher was a young man with a young family. Nancy hoped the war medicine would keep him safe in battle.

While Kingfisher hunted and made war, Nancy planted her fields of corn, pumpkins, beans, and peas. She gently poked holes in the earth, dropped in the seed, and with her foot covered the seed with dirt. She yanked up grass that choked the young plants and picked insects from their leaves and stems. She harvested, ground, and stored enough meal to feed her family for the coming winter. She worked in the commonly held fields to grow food for the sick and elderly.

Chores filled Nancy's days, but her children were close by and she had the company of other women. Together they tanned hides, collected herbs for medicines and dyes, strung nets across the river to catch fish, and made thread and cloth from bark and seeds. Nancy was happy, yet as time passed she grew lonely for Kingfisher. Restlessness also grew in her heart. Nancy knew the old songs, stories, and traditions. She knew farming, fishing, and foraging. She knew cooking, sewing, and childcare. But she had never traveled

Nancy Ward

beyond the Overhill Cherokee towns, and she knew nothing of the wars that occupied so much of the men's time.

In 1755, Nancy's restlessness led her to march to war with Kingfisher. A few women often went with war parties to help load weapons, lead packhorses, cook meals, and nurse the wounded. And in every generation, a handful of Cherokee women chose to paint themselves as warriors, take the stimulating black drink, and fight in battle. War Women were greatly honored by the People, but few chose this path. Women owned and were responsible for the villages, homes, fields, children, sick, and elderly. If too many women left to fight wars, there would be no one to tend to and manage these precious things. Nancy was not one of the few who chose this path. Instead, she traveled with the warriors as a helper.

When Ka-ti was almost three and Five Killer stopped nursing, Nancy made ready to embark on this adventure with her husband. Tame Doe agreed to care for the children while Nancy joined Kingfisher and 500 Cherokee warriors in a battle against the Creek. The Cherokee's ancient enemy claimed valuable hunting grounds in present-day Alabama, as did the Cherokee.

After the Chota Council decided to wage war, seven

The Cherokee Nation

days of preparation followed. A medicine man climbed to the top of the Council House at dawn to frighten away evil spirits. He roared like a bear and howled like a wolf. Seven days of fasting, cleansing, and dancing followed. Nancy listened and watched as the drum beats, like gunfire, accompanied the war dance. The dancers crouched, leapt, stomped, circled, spun, and shook spears, imitating warriors in the field. Black beads swung about their painted chests.

On the seventh day, the honored women prepared the sacred Black Drink in a clay pot. The women steeped the leaves and shoots of the bitter holly plant in simmering river water. Then, chanting a prayer, they threw salt on the fire and herbs into the pot. Finally, they submerged an entire branch of holly. The drink brewed for an hour as warriors danced the Eagle Tail dance to give them power. The movements showed how the eagle rests on the earth, then soars close to heaven. It was a dance of the opposites in the great circle of life—of male and female, summer and winter, heaven and earth, peace and war.

When the cleansing brew was black and bitter, each warrior took a turn drinking it from a polished pink conch shell. Afterward, they plunged into the Tennessee River as the priest shook black beads. He bid the

Nancy Ward

evil spirits to tear out their enemies' souls and seal them into a coffin sunk in deep black mud with a coiled serpent stationed above them.

Energized, the warriors shed all but their loincloths and gathered to head south. Scouts with wolf, owl, and fox skins draped about their shoulders went ahead to  watch for enemy ambushes. Oconostota and his captains mounted horses brought from the corrals beyond the fields. The war chief carried a red war club. His first-captain, Standing Turkey, carried a red flag. Surgeons and drummers followed, and then warriors on foot. Two priests carried a chest covered with deer hide that held sacred war medicine. No one but the priests could carry or open the chest, and it never touched the ground.

Nancy, the other women, and young gun boys were in the rear of the procession. They led horses loaded with more weapons and supplies. In Nancy's hair was a swan feather given to her by the honored women. Around her neck hung a wolf tooth to lend her power. In her pouch was a pinch of Chota soil, to keep her spirit close to her children and town. The journey was long, but Nancy was young and strong.

The Cherokee Nation

After long days, the enemy was sighted at Taliwa along the Coosa River. The warriors fanned out through the forest. Musket fire exploded and smoke billowed through the air as Nancy and Kingfisher crouched behind a half-rotten log. Nancy measured powder and chewed bullets so they would rip and tear the skin of the Cherokee's enemies. Red and black stripes and dots covered Kingfisher's face and naked chest. Tucked in his breechcloth was the blowgun the elders had taught him to use. Across his back was strung a bow and a bundle of arrows. But, like most warriors, Kingfisher now relied on English weapons and powder. The *Ani-kusa*, or Creek, also had powerful weapons, and they outnumbered the Cherokee.

Suddenly, a loud explosion threw Nancy to the ground. The Cherokee chief, Raven, fell wounded to the leafy forest floor. Through the haze, Nancy saw that Kingfisher lay crumbled on the ground nearby. A musket ball had torn open her young husband's chest.

Nancy bit her lip to keep from crying out. She tore a strip of cloth from her shawl and pressed it against the blood pouring from the gaping chest wound. Warriors rushed to cover Nancy as she tried to staunch the scarlet blood. But it seeped through the cloth and onto Kingfisher's chest like a mountain spring bub-

 Nancy Ward

bling up from the ground. Nancy knew there was no hope. She cradled Kingfisher's head on her lap and held his gunpowder-stained fingers in her own. As his spirit left his body, she whispered a prayer that it would travel safely to the spirit world.

The Creek warriors were advancing as Nancy watched Kingfisher die. The war captain commanded his warriors to gather the wounded and retreat. But Nancy knew that until Kingfisher's death was avenged, his spirit would wander the earth. According to nature's law, only the death of an enemy would allow Kingfisher's soul to enter the next world. Burying her grief, she let the spirit of the wolf fill her with courage. Nancy would not become a Creek captive and never see her children again. Nor would she allow Kingfisher's death to go unavenged. She picked up her young husband's gun, looked over the log, and fired at the advancing Creek warriors. The Cherokee warriors saw Kingfisher bleeding at Nancy's feet and took heart. A warrior near her let out a wail, then a wave of war cries rent through the air. They renewed their attack and pushed back the Creek attack.

After the battle, the warriors washed off their war paint in a frigid mountain stream and buried Kingfisher under a pile of rocks. On a large boulder, they

The Cherokee Nation

painted a picture of the Battle of Taliwa. A fish depicted a memorial to Kingfisher, and a black bird represented the wounding of Chief Raven. As a warning for the Creek, they painted a map that showed the boundaries of Cherokee territory—a line the Creek must not cross.

While the warriors painted the boulder and readied for the trip home, Nancy knelt by her young husband's grave. Above her, a blanket of twinkling stars filled the dark night sky. Once, brave young warriors like Kingfisher had chased a big dog away from an old couple's corn meal, the old ones said. The spirit dog flew to the sky—a place of serenity and open space. The dog trailed crumbs of meal that stayed in the sky showing where it traveled. The crumbs then turned into stars, which honored the brave young men. That night, Nancy knew, the stars honored Kingfisher.

Chapter Three

Beloved Woman

At the battle with the Creeks, Nancy had seen firsthand the glory and horror of war. She experienced both a warrior's thirst for revenge and a widow's grief. She had lost her young husband after only a few years together, and now her life would never again be the same.

Nancy returned to Chota with the war party. Before entering the town, they stopped and attached the scalps of fallen Creek warriors to red-painted poles and repainted themselves with black and red stripes and dots. Shouting war cries and brandishing their weapons, they entered the town. The residents of Chota ran cheering to greet them. The few Creek captives were taunted and jeered, then tied to poles in the town square. Nancy's thirst for revenge had lasted only through the Battle of Taliwa. For the sake of the

The Cherokee Nation

captives, she was thankful that Chota was a city of sanctuary where no one could be tortured or killed. The captives would only endure insults until the Council met to decide whether they should be adopted, enslaved, or ransomed back to the Creek.

"*Asiyu*," Nancy greeted her children, which meant, "Hello, I am good." But because she had touched blood, Nancy could not go home right away. Instead, she went to a small hut on the edge of town. Alone in a small room, she prayed, fasted, and cleansed her soul of hatred and violence. She saw no one but the honored women, who brought her food and drink.

Seven days later, Nancy walked home. When she arrived, Tame Doe came to her with exciting news. During Nancy's isolation, the Chota Council had met to discuss her courage. The Council decided to bestow on Nancy an honored post that had not been filled for a long time. Nancy would be named *Ghigha*, the Beloved Woman of the Cherokee.

Nancy was stunned, for past Ghigha's had been elders. But the councilors of Chota were convinced that the spirit of Selu, the Corn Goddess, spoke through seventeen-year-old Nancy. Once, Selu had been just a stalk of corn growing alone in the forest. Then she changed into a woman and became the mother of the

 Nancy Ward

Cherokee. As the spirit of Selu, Nancy became the mother of the People, too.

As Nancy awaited the ceremony to declare her the Cherokee Beloved Woman, the honored women and councilors told Nancy her duties. As Beloved Woman, Nancy would have to protect the People from harm, keep the laws of hospitality, and guide the People along the white road of peace. She would prepare the Black Drink of the warriors, determine the fates of prisoners, and have a vote on the Chota Council. At first, Nancy was bewildered by this great responsibility. But as the days passed, her courage grew. The Great Spirit had presented this challenge, and for the sake of her People she must face it.

The day when Nancy would be named Beloved Woman soon arrived. Tame Doe made Nancy a new white deerskin skirt and shawl for the ceremony. Tame Doe embroidered wolf teeth, shells, porcupine quills, and pearls onto the baby-soft white hide. Then she slipped copper bracelets and rings on Nancy's wrists and fingers and placed a crown made of swan feathers on her head.

Nancy sat with the honored women by the sacred fire in the Council House. Chief Oconostota rose and told of Nancy's bravery in the Taliwa battle. The

The Cherokee Nation

honored women spoke, too. They had seen the spirit of Selu in Nancy's thirst for knowledge and her kindness to others. Like the wolf, Nancy was a teacher and pathfinder, strong in herself, yet bound tightly to her clan and People.

Chief Little Carpenter spoke last, his eyes twinkling with happiness and pride. It had been a long time since the Cherokee had a Beloved Woman, he said. But wars engulfed the People more in each generation, and balance was sorely needed. Little Carpenter walked to Nancy, who rose to face him. "Through the Beloved Woman," the peace chief said, "the path is made white." Then Little Carpenter handed Nancy a white swan wing fan. She accepted it, and the People cheered.

At first, Nancy had few duties as Beloved Woman. The People were at peace, and the tribe prospered. She sat on the Council, ran her household, and watched her children grow. Nancy loved her children and wanted more.

A year after Kingfisher's death, Nancy began to look for a new husband. A Virginia trader who lived with the Cherokee caught her eye. The strapping Irishman named Bryant Ward had a full beard, a hearty laugh, and a pack train of twenty horses. Like most white people, he had the rude habit of looking directly

Nancy Ward

into people's eyes and speaking loudly as if the listeners were deaf. But he was honest and respected the People. He was also a good hunter. Nancy knew that Bryant Ward had a wife and family in Virginia whom he returned to every winter for a few months, but that did not bother her. Few Indian men could afford to keep two families in meat, but Bryant Ward could.

Many white traders and Cherokee women married to reinforce the trading ties between the English settlers and the tribe. Others married partners they loved and respected. For some couples, both were true. Bryant Ward admired Nancy's piercing black eyes and queenly manner. He also valued her high status in the tribe, for it would strengthen his own. Bryant and Nancy were married in the late 1750s and had a daughter, whom they named Betsy.

When meat grew less plentiful because of overhunting for furs, Bryant brought Nancy hogs from across the mountains. Nancy learned how to raise the hogs for meat and taught the People what she learned. Bryant also showed her how the white men turned over the soil with a plow and then planted crops in wide rows. This method was more efficient, he said, so more food could be grown.

Nancy discussed the white people's farming meth-

The Cherokee Nation

ods with the Women's Council. The honored women felt strongly that it was best to grow only what was needed and leave as much forest as possible to harbor the animals. The honored women also felt men did not belong in the fields and that slicing open the face of Mother Earth was unkind. For the time being, the honored women chose to continue the old ways.

Nancy had not been married to Bryant Ward very long when war again disrupted the People's lives. In what came to be known as the French and Indian War, the English and French fought for control of the lush Mississippi Valley. A stream of English and French ambassadors visited the Cherokee. The diplomats addressed the councils and asked for alliances. In return, both the French and English promised guns, powder, and other trade goods. Little Carpenter encouraged the Cherokee to support their longtime English friends.

Nancy agreed, but warned that Cherokee women, children, and elders would be unprotected if the warriors left to fight in the white men's war. The Council agreed with their Beloved Woman. The Cherokee would fight with the British against the French if forts were built in Cherokee country to protect civilians. The English agreed and built three forts in Cherokee

Nancy Ward

country. Fort Dobbs in North Carolina protected the middle towns. Fort Prince George on the Keowee River sat near the lower towns. Diamond-shaped Fort Loudoun was in Overhill country, where the Tellico River dumped into the Tennessee.

Fort Loudoun was only five miles north of Chota. While it was being built, Nancy often went with a group of villagers to watch. She and the Overhill women admired the fort's size and the pointed stakes, or "palisades," that surrounded it. But they clucked that the wooden barracks would be cold in the winter and hot in the summer, and they shuddered at how cruelly white officers treated militiamen who drank too much or disobeyed orders. A Cherokee chief could never inflict hundreds of lashes with a cat-o-nine tail on his own brothers.

Nancy felt sorry for the white soldiers and their wives and befriended them. The whites often became sick with illnesses that the Cherokee knew how to cure using the gifts of the forest. Nancy showed the wives and daughters of soldiers of the Fort Loudoun encampment how to make a drink from the evergreen spruce to ward off scurvy and where to dig for the root that cured snake bites. She showed them how to mix bear grease with goldenseal leaves to repel insects, use

The Cherokee Nation

Settlers built forts to protect themselves from Native American attacks.

 Nancy Ward

scarlet root to kill lice, and drink liverwort root tea to soothe coughs. The whites grew so fond of the energizing ginseng plant that it quickly became an important trading item. Before long, one of the man-shaped roots was worth two buckskins.

When Fort Loudoun was completed in 1757, soldiers and their families who had grown friendly with the Cherokee came to Chota to celebrate. In their honor, the Chota Town Council raised an English flag with its cross of St. George above the Council House. Alongside it flew Chota's white flag of peace. The feasting and dancing lasted for days, and the Chota women gave the whites hundreds of baskets of meat, cornbread, and squash to take home with them. Several days later, 700 Cherokee warriors left to fight the French with the British redcoats and the Virginia and South Carolina militias.

The following spring, the warriors returned to Chota, half-starved and disgusted. Nancy listened with concern as Dragging Canoe made his report to the Chota Council. The warriors had fought with the British at French Fort Duquesne along the Ohio River. But William Pitt and John Forbes, the British commanders, did not know how to fight in the American wilderness. And they refused to listen to Cherokee

The Cherokee Nation

advice. Instead of taking cover behind trees and cliffs, the foolish redcoats marched noisily up to their enemy in open fields. The French, Dragging Canoe said, had been far wiser. They listened to their Shawnee allies and fought with craft, stealth, and skill. Together, the French and Shawnee had mowed the British down in a series of humiliating losses. After many defeats, the disgusted Cherokee warriors had packed up their gear and stumbled home.

But Dragging Canoe had much worse news to report than the arrogance of British officers. The officers had bought, sold, and traded the Cherokee like slaves, he said, and fed them skimpy rations of wormy and rotten corn. And then, when the warriors lost their own horses in battle, the officers refused to replace them. Infuriated, Dragging Canoe and a hundred other warriors had taken horses to replace the ones they had lost and left for home. The British called the Cherokee deserters and horse thieves and hunted them down. Nineteen warriors were killed and scalped.

Nancy had never seen Dragging Canoe so furious. The insults were too many, Nancy's cousin said. He was going to avenge the dead warriors. The Chota Council tried to calm Dragging Canoe and his young, angry followers. But they took to the warpath without the approval of Council. The renegade band attacked frontier homesteads and settlements and did not stop until they had killed nineteen whites to avenge and release the souls of their dead friends. The raids turned some frontier settlers who had been friendly into die-hard Indian haters.

Nancy feared the returning warriors' rash attacks would create a snake pit of trouble, and it did. Grim messages soon arrived from the British. They threatened to attack Cherokee towns with a large army and cut off all guns and supplies to the People. The French, seeing the breech between the English and Cherokee, quickly sent ambassadors to the middle and lower towns. Ambassador Lantagnac told the People they needed French help to withstand a British assault. Grabbing a war hatchet, the French ambassador struck a painted pole and cried: "Who is there that will take the hatchet for the King of France. Let him come forward." Chief Saloue of a middle town grabbed the hatchet and said, "I will take it." Wauhatchie, the chief of three lower towns, did the same.

Although each Cherokee town governed itself, in the past they had fought common enemies together. Now they were divided. The Overhill towns clung to their deep friendship with the English. Nancy's task was to walk the white road of peace, and she argued that alliance with the French would destroy the Cherokee. The only wise path, she said, was to stay neutral in the white men's wars. Rebellious Dragging Canoe railed against Nancy and the Overhill town leaders. He left with his brothers and other young warriors to join the lower and middle towns that sided with the French. As Nancy had feared, the bloody French-Cherokee raids brought swift and terrible British revenge. Nearly 2,000 well-armed soldiers gathered in Charles Town, South Carolina, to march on the Cherokee.

Nancy had killed in war and did not fear it. She knew a warrior's death was honorable. But she was responsible for the survival of the tribe and the well being of all the People, especially women, children, and elders. In the Chota Council, Nancy pushed hard for diplomatic solutions.

In 1760, the Chota Council sent two peace delegations to Virginia and South Carolina to convince the white leaders that Chota remained neutral. Little Carpenter traveled to Winchester, Virginia, to meet with Royal Governor Dinwiddie. "The beloved headsman of Chota sits under a white flag and wishes to preserve it from blood," Little Carpenter told the governor. Meanwhile, Nancy traveled with Oconostota to meet

 Nancy Ward

with Lyttleton, the Royal Governor of South Carolina.

Bustling Charles Town impressed Nancy, who had never been away from the mountains before. At last she saw the ocean, carriages, and tall stone buildings like Little Carpenter had seen in London. The women's silk and satin dresses—more colorful than the brightest birds and flowers of the forest hills—amazed her. Nancy was more convinced than ever that the British were a very powerful people.

There was not much time for exploring, however. The entourage was quickly ushered into the state house to meet Governor Lyttleton. Oconostota stepped forward and began to speak in his measured manner. Nancy learned quickly that the governor was not accustomed to women leaders. Lyttleton glared at Nancy, then interrupted Oconostota in the rude way of some white men. Sharply, the governor asked Chief Oconostota why he had brought a woman to such important talks. Puzzled, Oconostota answered with a question of his own: "Why are there no English women at the meeting? It is customary among red men to admit women to our councils. As the white people, as well as the red, are born of women, it not that the custom among them, also?" The governor swallowed his irritation and gestured for the chief to continue.

The Cherokee Nation

Oconostota spoke words of peace. He reminded the governor of the Cherokee's long friendship with the English and explained that the Cherokee were now divided. The Overhill towns remained committed to friendship with England, yet no longer wished to join their war against the French. Meanwhile, many of the middle and lower towns had allied with the French. "There has been bad doings at the Towns hereabouts, but I was not the beginner of them," Oconostota said to the grim-faced governor. "The path has been a little bad, but I am come to make it straight. There has been blood spilled, but I am come to clean it up. I am a warrior, but I want no war with the English."

After he spoke, Nancy walked forward and laid a peace offering of deer skins before the governor. Lyttleton did not look at Nancy or nod his thanks. "I have permitted you to lay down those skins," he said scowling. "But I do not accept them in token of the peace you propose. If any Cherokee fight against the British, all Cherokee are the enemy." The governor then ordered soldiers to escort the peace delegation under heavy guard to Fort Prince George near the lower Cherokee towns in South Carolina. Nancy was later released, but twenty-eight chiefs were imprisoned in a room barely large enough to hold ten men.

 Nancy Ward

By long tradition, peace delegates were guaranteed safe passage to and from their homes. News of this grave insult to the People spread quickly. Little Carpenter, home from Virginia, hurried to Fort Prince George to talk to Lyttleton. The governor agreed to free the chiefs, but only if the tribe surrendered an equal number of warriors to be executed. Horrified, Little Carpenter explained that was impossible. The governor made a new offer. If Little Carpenter signed an agreement promising that the entire tribe would again fight with the English against the French, the governor would free Oconostota and two other chiefs.

Desperate to free at least a few Cherokee leaders, Little Carpenter agreed. Once freed, Oconostota let his fury fly. He railed against the treacherous English, adamantly foregoing peace in favor of retaliation. Nancy and Little Carpenter again counseled for patience and negotiation, but Oconostota joined forces with Dragging Canoe and attacked Fort Prince George. After the warriors ambushed the fort's commander and surrounded the fort, the soldiers inside slaughtered the remaining Cherokee chiefs. Oconostota sent word of the murders throughout Cherokee country, and raiding parties began terrorizing white homesteads and settlements throughout the land. Only when

The Cherokee Nation

a large British army marched toward the fort did Oconostota end the siege.

Nancy and Little Carpenter were horrified, but their cries for peace were drowned out by the desire for revenge. The Overhill towns joined the middle and lower towns in taking up the hatchet against the British. Nancy's Uncle Willenawah led a Cherokee army to Fort Loudoun near Chota, where forewarned settlers and a small garrison of soldiers waited behind a locked gate. Other bands of warriors ravaged frontier settlements throughout the Land of the Blue Smoke.

Nancy feared that angry warriors would kill her white husband and other whites living with the Overhill Cherokee. Quickly, she helped them escape to the forts and settlements east of the mountains. Then she gathered the Cherokee civilians of the Overhill towns and led them to safety in the high mountains. In the forest, the women, children, and elders killed what small game they could find and gathered wild nuts and fruit. Nancy and the other women worried about their untended crops but did not dare return to town.

The refugees were as divided as the warriors. Some supported the attacks on the English forts. But Nancy and others were friends and relatives of the frontier soldiers and civilians. Nancy organized a group of

women to take food to the outnumbered and besieged settlers at Fort Loudoun. Nancy's Uncle Willenawah watched, horrified, as the women marched boldly up to the walls of the fort with baskets of food. From inside the fort, the settlers threw over ropes and pulled up the baskets. As the women passed the warriors on their way back to their mountain camps, Nancy's Uncle Willenawah shook black beads at them. But the women held their heads high and walked on. While Cherokee women breathed, their friends and families would not starve.

Yet the women's meager offerings could not stave off the hunger of the Fort Loudoun residents. After a long, hot summer, they asked the Cherokee for terms of surrender. Once again, Nancy lobbied for humane treatment, and the chiefs agreed not to take whites captive. Instead, the soldiers and civilians would be allowed to walk over the mountains with only enough guns and powder to hunt on their journey. The gate was thrown open, and the bedraggled residents of the fort hurried away.

Nancy was relieved that the standoff with the soldiers had ended. But the trouble at Fort Loudoun was not over. Whooping victory calls, Cherokee warriors entered the fort to gather the guns and ammunition that

The Cherokee Nation

the English had promised to leave behind. Inside the fort, they became suspicious when they found only a few weapons. A more thorough search revealed that many guns and much of the powder had been buried. This violated the terms of surrender, and the warriors were furious. As the warriors chased after the English, their war cries filled the air. In a surprise attack, they killed twenty-five soldiers—the same number of chiefs killed inside Fort Prince George.

Chapter Four

Respite

That fall and winter, Nancy and other Cherokee civilians learned for the first time just how devastating a white army's revenge could be. Word arrived that Colonel James Grant was leading a force of 2,600 soldiers to attack the Cherokee towns. Nancy led the Cherokee civilians deeper into the Smoky Mountains. The Cherokee warriors fought bravely and took scalps. But the soldiers were better armed and took more. Fifteen of the middle and lower Cherokee towns were destroyed.

The white soldiers burned Cherokee houses and rode horses over their crops. They smashed the large gourds filled with bear fat and acorn oil and stole the People's winter stores of wild potatoes, dried berries, and squash. They tore winter clothing to shreds and slaughtered the dogs and livestock. The suffering this caused was the worst Nancy had ever seen. Wintertime roots could not sustain 5,000 cold and homeless Cherokee People. Desperate Cherokee chiefs traveled to South Carolina and Virginia and signed treaties promising to support the British.

By 1763, the British had at last driven the French from the Mississippi Valley, and King George III issued a proclamation forbidding American colonists to buy or settle on land west of the Appalachian Mountains. The King's agent to the Cherokee, John Stuart, said Britain wanted peace on the frontier and good trading with the People.

Good trading was out of the question, however, for war had taken a heavy toll. The loss of crops, orchards, tools, and weapons hit the Cherokee hard, and Nancy had her hands full trying to repair the damage. Her task became harder when another small pox epidemic hit and weakened the People further. But Nancy did not lose hope. The Cherokee were strong and had survived much. White settlers had been slowly pushing into the mountains, yet the tribe still controlled 43,000 square miles of land in the Carolinas, Georgia, and Tennessee. If the English obeyed their king's law, the Cherokee could regain their strength and live forever in the land of their ancestors.

Nancy Ward

But land-hungry veterans of the French and Indian War did not honor their king's law or Cherokee claims. Colonial militias gave veterans grants for western land in exchange for their military service. Land-hungry whites began to beat paths along the rivers and through the mountain passes to Cherokee land. When the settlers refused to leave, colonial and British agents in charge of Indian Affairs told the Cherokee to give away the settled lands in order to keep the peace. Many Cherokee warriors wanted to fight, but the People had to focus all their energy toward ensuring their survival.

To escape these hard times, a few thousand Cherokee refugees traveled west for the wilderness across the Mississippi River. Thousands more refugees from the destroyed middle and lower towns fled to the Overhill towns. Nancy parceled out food to the refugees and collected hemp, nettles, milkweed, and grasses to weave cloth for clothes and blankets. The men went in search of game for meat. But the new white settlers along the Holston, Nolichucky, Watauga, Clinch, and New Rivers hunted also, and there was not enough to go around. Scant game also meant fewer furs to trade for supplies. The People began to buy food, clothing, and seed from white traders on credit. When the unpaid bills mounted, the People were forced to settle

The Cherokee Nation

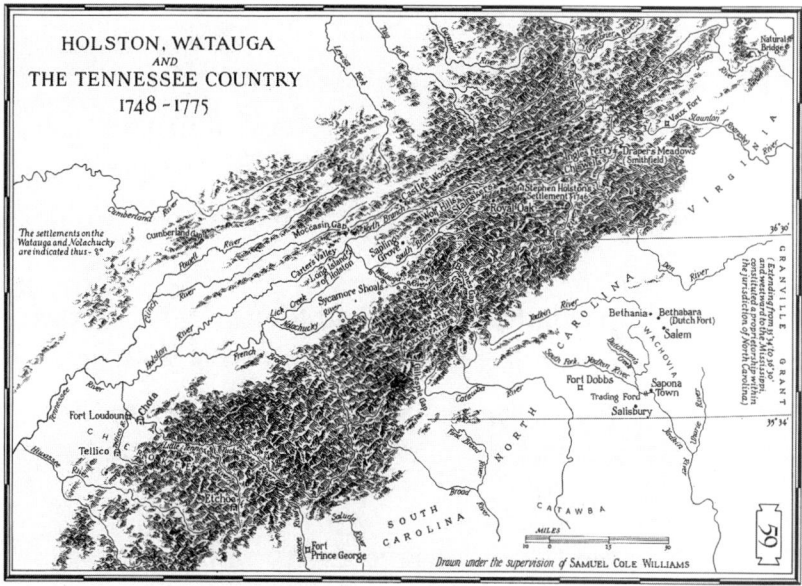

Forced to give more and more land to white settlers, the Cherokee claim in the Western Frontier changed drastically in the eighteenth century.

their debts by signing away more and more Cherokee land.

Nancy dealt with daily crises and threw herself into helping her tribe prosper again. More than ever before, the Cherokee depended on farming and foraging for wild foods. In the fall, she and her children gathered hickory nuts and tapped maple trees to make syrup. In the spring and summer, they gathered strawberries in the open meadows and climbed the foothills to pick blackberries, wild grapes, and persimmons.

Nancy and the other Cherokee women replanted

Nancy Ward

and expanded their fields of squash, beans, and corn. No part of the corn crop went unused. The women ground yellow, red, and blue kernels into meal for making bread and porridge. They beat young corn to a pulp to dress skins and used the smoke from burning corncobs to tan them. The corn juice they saved to drink, to erase tattoo marks, and to prime the insides of pottery before it was fired. The women also added fields of tobacco for trading. To improve their yields, Nancy allowed Bryant to turn over ground with his horse and plow.

Slowly, the Cherokee recovered from the devastation wrought by the French and Indian War. The Overhill Cherokee began to trade and visit with nearby whites, now called the Overmountain settlers. At Jacob Brown's trading post along the Nolichucky River, Nancy traded extra crops, handmade baskets, and medicinal roots for calico fabric, buttons, metal tools, and iron kettles. On these trips, she got to know the Bean, Russell, and Shelby families. Nancy discussed farming and traded recipes with the white women. Their children played together outside.

As Nancy's friendships with neighboring whites deepened, many Cherokee men grew more resentful of the white presence as game grew even scarcer and

The Cherokee Nation

the fur trade suffered. Chiefs of the towns met and decided to contact Alexander Cameron, Deputy British Superintendent to the Cherokee. Cameron agreed to command the American colonists to leave the mountains, but the frontier people ignored his order. After that, Nancy and Little Carpenter had to work harder to maintain the peace.

Finally, the Overhill Cherokee came up with a scheme they hoped would solve the problem. They would rent land to the nearby whites for ten years. The white settlers agreed and paid the rent in guns, powder, and other much-needed trade goods. Nancy listened as Little Carpenter told the Overmountain whites what he expected in return for their generosity: "I expect friendship and good usage from my white brothers," the aging peace chief said. "It is but a little spot of ground, and I am willing that your people should live upon it. I pity the white people, but they do not pity me . . . The great Being above is very good, and provides for everybody. He gave us this land, but the white people seem to want to drive us from it."

Little Carpenter's speech to the Overmountain settlers expressed what Nancy herself felt. She liked her white friends, yet knew many were consumed by greed for land and had strange, unshakable notions about the

 Nancy Ward

People. The Cherokee farmed, had permanent villages, and governed themselves much as whites did. But many whites were convinced the Indians were savages. The Cherokee believed the Great Spirit was everywhere—in the air they breathed and water they drank. But settlers called them heathens for not worshipping the white man's God, who lived inside churches. It was true that Cherokee people sometimes did bad things, such as when unruly young men got in fights and stole horses. But usually they were drunk on liquor given to them by the whites. More than once, drunken men of the Overhill had threatened to kill whites living among them. Sometimes, Nancy hid the white men in her house until they could be safely escorted home. Still, Nancy did not give up hope that they could learn to get along and share the land in peace.

Chapter Five

Division

As Nancy had hoped, by the late 1700s, the relationship between the Cherokee and the white settlers had begun to stabilize. Nancy was pleased by her people's expanding fields that made them less dependent on hunting. But the Cherokee had fought a war with the Chickasaws that used up almost all of the Nation's weapons, and now they were vulnerable to attack. The Chota Council was seeking a solution to this problem when a land speculator named Richard Henderson visited Chota in 1774. Henderson told the Council that his Transylvania Land Company wanted to buy 20 million acres in what later would become Kentucky and part of Tennessee. The company would divide the Cumberland Valley into smaller parcels and sell them to frontier families.

The Cherokee met with Henderson in March 1775

Nancy Ward

at Sycamore Shoals at the headwaters of the Tennessee River. Nancy Ward, Little Carpenter, Oconostota, Dragging Canoe, and 1,000 Cherokee gathered to meet with "Carolina Dick" Henderson. The Chota chiefs, chosen to represent the tribe, spoke in favor of the deal. But grumbling erupted among the group of warriors. Nancy's cousin Dragging Canoe, whose only resemblance to his father Little Carpenter was his pockmarked face, was their leader. Now the war chief of Great Island Town, he rose to his full height of six feet and spoke angrily:

> We have, in the past, left tombs of our ancestors behind. Entire nations of native people have melted away like balls of snow in the sun. We had hoped that the white men would not be willing to travel beyond the mountains. Now that hope is gone. They have passed the mountains and settled upon Cherokee land. They wish to have that sanctioned by treaty. When that is gained, the same encroaching spirit will lead them upon other lands of the Cherokees. Finally, the whole country, which the Cherokees and their fathers have so long occupied, will be demanded, and the remnant of the Ani-Yunwiya, once so great and formidable, will be compelled to seek refuge in some distant wilderness, until they again behold

The Cherokee Nation

the advancing banners of the same greedy host. Not being able to point out any further retreat for the miserable Cherokees, the extinction of the whole race will be proclaimed. Should we not therefore run all risks, and incur all consequences, rather than submit to further laceration of our country. Such treaties may be all right for men who are too old to hunt or fight. As for me, I have my young warriors about me. We will have our lands. A-waninski, I have spoken.

When Dragging Canoe ended his speech, the crowd stood in stunned silence. Nancy was greatly stirred, as were the chiefs who had favored the deal. Raven sensed the mood of the People had changed, and declared the negotiations over. The People turned away quietly to pack for the journey home. Henderson, realizing that the rich Cumberlands were about to slip through his fingers, quickly promised a final feast. Sides of beef and pork, bread pudding with raisins, wheat bread, wine, and rum were served. The Cherokee stayed to eat, drink, and dance. Hours later, Henderson played his trump card to the sated crowd. He lead the Cherokee to a cabin and threw open the door to reveal twice the booty he had offered before. The impact of Dragging Canoe's speech had worn off,

 Nancy Ward

and the chiefs could not resist. An agreement was made ready for signing.

Nancy watched solemnly as Oconostota approached an old tree stump that served as a table. On it was a piece of paper outlining the terms. But before he could sign it, Henderson said the Cherokee must give up two more parcels of land, as well. The first was a "path" through Cherokee country to the Cumberlands. The second gave the Overhill settlers along the Watauga River ownership of the land they now rented from the People. Dismay and resignation showed on the faces of Nancy and the chiefs. Fed up by these last-minute demands, Dragging Canoe leapt to his feet and shouted: "We have given you this. Why do you ask for more? There is no more game left between the Watauga and the Cumberland. There is a cloud hanging over it. You will find it is a dark and bloody ground."

As Dragging Canoe and his followers stormed off, a chill ran down Nancy's spine. She feared her cousin's prophecy, but believed the whites were vast and all-powerful like the great ocean leading to England and France. Nancy remained convinced that only peaceful coexistence with whites would ensure Cherokee survival. The weary chiefs took the goods Henderson offered, and Oconostota signed the treaty with a black

The Cherokee Nation

X. As he signed, Nancy looked back to see the renegade warriors climbing into long dugout canoes and shoving off down the river. Dragging Canoe headed the group and left without looking back.

Nancy returned to her life in Chota, and the renegades settled where Chickamauga Creek ran into the Tennessee River, near present day Chattanooga. They took their new name from this place, calling themselves the "Chickamauga." Later they moved to the foot of Lookout Mountain beyond tortuous rapids that sucked and whirled and provided protection from sudden attacks.

Dragging Canoe and Nancy Ward traveled opposite paths. Dragging Canoe turned his back on the negotiations, compromises, and concessions that had cost the Cherokee so much. He embraced war as the only honorable choice and set about trying to drive white colonists off the southern Appalachian frontier. Meanwhile, Nancy concentrated on saving lives, homes, crops, and towns. Only this, she believed, would ensure the survival of her outnumbered and outgunned People.

In 1776, Nancy's task grew more difficult because of the rift between the American colonists and their British rulers. Once again, two warring parties of whites pressured the Cherokee to choose sides. Both the Cherokee and Chickamauga received delegations, accepted gifts, and listened to rosy promises. The frontier colonists—most of whom sided with the revolutionaries—promised a new spirit of cooperation, friendship, and trade after American Independence. Nancy's heart was with her frontier friends. Dragging Canoe, however, cast his lot with the British, who promised to remove white colonists from Indian lands once and for all.

From the British, the Chickamauga received 300 packhorses loaded with guns and ammunition. The British master plan called for the Chickamauga to attack the frontier backdoor with the help of other Indian allies and loyalist colonists. At the same time, the British navy would assault the Atlantic seacoast. A determined Dragging Canoe traveled through the middle and lower towns recruiting more warriors: "The white men have almost surrounded us, leaving only a little spot of ground to stand upon," he told them. "It seems to be their intention to destroy us as a nation. As for me, I have a great many of my young warriors around me, and they mean to have their lands."

That winter, the Chickamauga attacked white settle-

The Cherokee Nation

ments and forts from Virginia to Georgia. Meanwhile, Nancy and the Chota Council debated what to do. At first, the Peace Chief and the Beloved Woman convinced the Overhill Cherokee to remain neutral. But in the spring of 1776, false rumors flew that a large American force, angered by the Chickamauga raids, was marching to destroy *all* the Cherokee towns. About the same time, an impressive delegation of unified, British-allied chiefs arrived in Chota. The Iroquois, Mohawk, Delaware, Ottawa, Shawnee, and Mingo chiefs convened at an event called the "Grand Talks" with leaders from all the Cherokee towns. The delegation of visiting chiefs proposed the Cherokee join with them and the British to drive the American frontier army back east across the Appalachians. The chiefs gave speeches and offered war belts decorated with conch and clamshells to the Cherokee chiefs.

The revered Shawnee chief, Cornstalk, said the American war against King George III was a great opportunity for all the native peoples. The English king had brought trade and told his American children not to steal the Indians' land. But the American colonists stole it anyway. His own Shawnee tribe, Cornstalk said, once possessed land reaching almost to the seashore, but now had hardly enough ground to stand

 Nancy Ward

on. "The lands where the Shawnee have but lately hunted are covered with forts and armed men," Cornstalk said. "When a fort appears, you may depend upon it, there will soon be towns and settlements of white men. It is plain that the white people intend to wholly destroy the Indians. It is better for the red men to die like warriors than to diminish away by inches. The cause of the red men is just, and I hope that the Great Spirit who governs everything will favor us."

Cornstalk ended his talk by pouring red paint over his nine-foot, purple war belt. Nancy knew that peace was now broken. When Cornstalk held out the belt for acceptance, silence filled the Council House. Dragging Canoe rose, took it in his hands and raised it high over his head. As he did, a Cherokee Chief named Osioota jumped from his seat and cried: "Death to the Unakas!" Throwing back his head, Osioota sang the Cherokee war song as others began to beat the drums:

> Wherever the earth is lit by the sun,
> Moon shines by night, grass grows or waters run,
> Be't known that we are going, like afar,
> In hostile fields to wage destructive war,
> Like men we go, to meet our Country's foes,
> Who woman-like, shall fly our dreaded blows,

The Cherokee Nation

But when we go, who knows which shall return,
When growing dangers rise with each new morn,
Farewell, ye little ones, yet tender wives,
For you alone we would conserve our lives!
But cease to mourn, 'tis unavailing pain,
If not fore doom'd, we soon shall meet again.
But O ye friends! In case your comrades fall
Think that on our deaths for vengeance call
With upraid'd tomahawks pursue our blood,
And stain, with hostile streams, the conscious wood,
That pointing enemies may never tell the boasted
   place
Where we, their victims, fell.

Chief Cornstalk

 ## Nancy Ward

The drums grew louder as old and young men rose to dance. Doublehead, Young Tassel, Dragging Canoe, and the Raven of Chota led the People in frenzied twirling and stomping. Their bodies swayed and feet pounded faster and faster as they circled the Council House. Dragging Canoe held Cornstalk's great purple belt over his head as he danced. Nancy did not join the celebrating. She and Little Carpenter sat and watched in dejected silence. They feared for their white friends and recalled earlier encounters with huge armies—the burned towns, ruined crops, and hungry mouths.

After the foreign chiefs' visit, both the Cherokee and Chickamauga towns voted to attack the Patriot militias of the American frontier. Nancy was outvoted and unhappy. Yet she had a duty as Ghigha to protect the warriors, and she honored it. Before the assembled townspeople, Nancy stood by the fire in her gown trimmed in swans' down. The flickering firelight cast shadows on the Council House wall. Nancy grimly filled a giant clay pot with water, holly leaves, and roots. Between each movement, she swept her swans' wing fan over the drink and sang songs to protect the warriors in battle. Moving slowly around the fire, Nancy threw handfuls of salt in the pot, in the flames, and at the feet of the warriors.

The Cherokee Nation

After the warriors drank, they turned away to dance and sing. Nancy crept through the hollow log entrance to the Council House. Once again she hurried off to help her white friends. Nancy's husband, Bryant, was not in town during the Grand Talks. But her friend Isaac Thomas and three other white traders were. They had been seized and thrown into a stockade. Nancy knew that when war fever reached its pitch, her friends might be tortured or killed despite Chota's laws forbidding violence. She threw a rope over the prison walls and helped the men escape.

Nancy whispered to Isaac Thomas that peace was lost, but her friendship remained firm. "The same house shelters us, and the same sky covers us all," Nancy said. By mid-July, she warned the traders, Old Abram would lead 700 warriors to attack the Overmountain settlements. At the same time, Dragging Canoe would attack settlements around Long Island on the Holston River with a thousand warriors.

# Chapter Six

Long Island Treaty

As Nancy had instructed, the white traders rushed her warning of the upcoming attack to the settlers, and the news spread like brush fire through the southern frontier. The settlers had plenty of time to pack valuables and flock to the safety of nearby forts. The warriors set out on their campaign and returned deeply discouraged. With the other members of Chota's Council, Nancy listened impassively to the reports of the returning war parties.

Fort Caswell on the Watauga River had been filled with settlers from along Nolichucky, Watauga, and Holston rivers, Old Abram reported. The fort had been well supplied with food, livestock, militiamen, and weapons, and the Overhill warriors had been unable to scale the walls. During one attempt, the women of the fort had poured boiling water from washtubs onto

The Cherokee Nation

their heads. The discouraged and humiliated warriors retreated and returned home without a single scalp and only one captive. Nancy was glad no one was wounded or killed but dismayed that the captive was her old friend Mrs. Bean. She had been captured while driving her herd of cows to the fort.

Nancy's worry turned to dismay as Dragging Canoe reported on his army's dire fate at Long Island, near present-day Bridgeport, Alabama. The Americans had ambushed Dragging Canoe's army in a sudden militia attack, he said, killing thirteen warriors and wounding several more. After receiving a bullet wound in each thigh, Dragging Canoe was helped to his feet by two of his war captains. The warriors came home without a single scalp.

The Council adjourned to digest the bad news, and Nancy rushed to the neighboring town of Toqua to release her friend. The angry warriors wanted revenge, Nancy knew, and Mrs. Bean was their only spoil of war. She would have to hurry, for Toqua was not a city of refuge like Chota. Nancy grabbed her white swans' wing fan, ran to the corrals on the edge of town, and jumped astride a horse. Just in time, she galloped into Toqua's central square.

The crowd parted as Nancy rode through. She

Nancy Ward

jumped down off the horse and walked toward her terrified friend. Mrs. Bean was tied to a red painted post, and stacks of dry wood were heaped at her feet. As a warrior prepared to ignite the wood, Nancy approached. "As Beloved Woman, I demand that you stop," she said. She held her fan high in the air so everyone could see. The warrior scowled, but stepped back. Nancy kicked away the wood, cut Mrs. Bean free, and led her home to Chota.

In Chota, the neat log homes, fields, and livestock surprised Mrs. Bean. The town looked much like established white settlements, she said, only there were no cows. Nancy explained that Cherokee warriors believed that eating the fleet-footed deer helped them run swiftly. But to eat the lazy cow would make them slow. Mrs. Bean convinced Nancy this was false and explained the great benefits of having cows. Herds of beef meant a ready supply of meat year round. Cows also made milk, which could be made into cheese, cream, and butter. With Mrs. Bean's help, Nancy bought two cows and began raising her own herd.

As Nancy had feared, Americans were quick to seek revenge against the Cherokee for their attacks. In the fall of 1777, scouts brought word that a large force of American rebels was on the march. The frontier mi-

The Cherokee Nation

litias burned thirty-six hastily abandoned lower and middle Cherokee towns to ashes and pursued the vastly outnumbered townspeople into the mountains. Eighty men, women, and children were killed in the attacks. Then the American soldiers marched over Chimney Top Mountain toward the Overhill towns.

When news of the white army's approach arrived, a colossal debate erupted in the Chota Council. The Council blamed its troubles on the renegade Chickamaugas, but felt the only choice left was to fight. Nancy and Little Carpenter predicted the slaughter of the People if war was waged and begged the Council to pursue peace. Caleb Star, a white trader and friend of Nancy's, asked to speak. "Make peace with Christians," he urged. "The Cherokee cannot hope to defeat such a large force. The Great Spirit has foreordained that the White men will triumph over the Red men, and resistance will be futile."

The Overhill Cherokee listened to Nancy, Little Carpenter, and Caleb Star. A message was sent to the commanders of the advancing frontier armies, John Sevier, and William Christian. The Overhill Cherokee regretted the earlier attacks, the message read, and did not support Dragging Canoe's alliance with the British. For the first time, the Overhill Cherokee also

 Nancy Ward

informed on the Chickamaugas and told Sevier and Christian that Dragging Canoe planned to ambush them on the French Broad River. With this act, the split between the Cherokee and the Chickamauga widened.

The message from the Overhill Cherokee stopped the frontier armies from attacking their towns, but the Americans demanded that the Cherokee come to a treaty meeting at Long Island. One thousand Cherokee obeyed and met the Indian agents of Virginia and North Carolina at Long Island in July 1777. Hundreds of area settlers came, too. Some of the Americans wanted revenge for Cherokee attacks and burned with hatred for all Indians. Others had deep bonds of friendship and kinship with the Cherokee and wanted to live in peace.

Nancy was pleased when the American Indian agents in charge of the negotiations at Long Island showed great respect for the aging Chiefs Oconostota and Little Carpenter. The agents presented the chiefs with matching red coats trimmed with lace and seated them in two carved high-back chairs. The war and peace chiefs thanked the Indian agents for the honor, but said they were too old to speak for the Cherokee. Old Tassel, who had followed Little Carpenter as peace chief, addressed the gathering. Old Tassel knew

The Cherokee Nation

that for sparing the Overhill towns, the Americans would demand more Cherokee land. Nancy's heart nearly broke as Old Tassel addressed this injustice in a sad and measured way:

> When we enter into treaties with our father, the white people, their whole cry is more land. Indeed, it had seemed a formality with them to demand what they know we dare not refuse . . . You marched into our towns with a superior force. Your numbers far exceeded us, and we fled to the stronghold of our woods, there to secure our women and children. Our towns were left to your mercy. You killed a few scattered and defenseless individuals, spread fire and desolation wherever you pleased. Much has been said of what you term want of civilization among the Indians. Proposals have been made to us to adopt your laws, your religion, your manners, and your customs. We do not see the wisdom of that . . . You say, 'Why do not the Indians till the ground and live as we do?' May we not ask with equal propriety, 'Why do not the white people hunt and live as we do?' We wish, however, to be at peace with you, and to do as we would be done by. We do not quarrel with you for the killing of an occasional buffalo or deer on our lands, but your

 Nancy Ward

people go much further. They hunt to gain a livelihood. They kill all our game. But it is very criminal in our young men if they chance to kill a cow or a hog for their sustenance when they happen to be in your land? The Great Sprit has placed us in different situations. He had given you many advantages, but he had not created us to be your slaves. We are a separate people! He had stocked your lands with cows; ours with buffalo; yours with hogs, ours with bears; yours with sheep, ours with deer. He has given you the advantage that your animals are tame, while ours are wild and demand not only a larger space for range, but art to hunt and kill them. They are, nevertheless, as much our property as other animals are yours, and ought not to be taken from us without our consent, or for something of equal value.

Old Tassel's speech also moved the Indian agents, who rewrote the treaty to take less land than originally planned. But the Cherokee still gave up lands east of the Blue Ridge in South Carolina and in northeastern Tennessee. The People also promised not to fight for Britain. In return, the Americans promised a large shipment of food, farming supplies, and other goods to help the destitute Cherokee get back on their feet.

The Cherokee Nation

The Long Island Treaty was signed on July 4, 1777, and a spirit of renewed friendship reigned. A year earlier the American rebels had signed the Declaration of Independence from Britain, so an anniversary celebration was held. The soldiers paraded and fired two rounds. Whiskey was served, and the Cherokee danced. William Christian gave a speech: "Brothers, just one year ago the 13 United States declared themselves free and independent, and that they would no longer be in subjection and slavery to the King of Great Britain . . . we hope our brothers, the Cherokee, will now rejoice and be merry with us."

The next day, everyone left Long Island, except one white man. The states of Virginia and North Carolina had appointed frontiersman Joseph Martin an agent to the Cherokee. At the treaty site, Martin built a large log home and storehouse to hold the goods owed to the People. Before long, he asked a young Cherokee

Cherokee Peace Pipe.

 Nancy Ward

woman he had met to marry him: Betsy Ward, the daughter of Nancy and Bryant Ward. After the marriage, Nancy's family ties to the Americans ran even deeper than before. Joseph Martin was accepted as a full member of the Wolf Clan.

Nancy's hopes for peace remained high, but were dashed when the Americans suffered many military defeats early in the Revolution. The supplies the Americans had promised to the Cherokee did not arrive, and the Overhill towns strained to feed and house the thousands of refugees from the middle and lower towns. When children began whimpering with hunger and nursing women's milk dried in their breasts, Nancy slaughtered her cows to feed the weakest. She kept only enough cattle to breed new calves for the future. Nancy also called for a gathering of the People to do the dance of charity.

Ragged people came with meager offerings from their encampments in the forest. One by one, with tomahawks in hand, warriors acted out how they took their first scalps. As each man ended his dance, he threw onto a blanket a small bag of cornmeal, a piece of meat, a string of wampum, or piece of clothing. The offerings were divided between the poorest widows and children, but it was not nearly enough. Entire

The Cherokee Nation

families ranged about woods desperately seeking game, digging for roots, and scrounging for berries. Cherokee men, humiliated that their families were reduced to living like animals, left to join the British-allied Chickamaugas.

Chapter Seven

Concessions

In May of 1780, Bryant Ward returned from a trading trip with the news that British General Cornwallis had bombarded and now occupied Charles Town. Chickamauga messengers soon brought more news. Great shiploads of guns, ammunition, seed, food, and cloth were docked at the British supply depot in Augusta, Georgia. Supplies were free for the taking for all Cherokee who fought against the frontier Americans. Nancy objected, but desperation forced the Council to once again take the British and Chickamaugas by the hand. Later, Thomas Jefferson wrote that the Overhill Cherokee's "distress was allowed to continue too long. It was natural that it developed into a head when we did nothing to help them meet their needs."

The British demanded a steep price for their sup-

The Cherokee Nation

plies. While the Chickamaugas attacked Nashborough and remote Cumberland Valley settlements, the Overhill Cherokee must attack the Watauga and Nolichucky militias—the Overmountain Settlement. With a heavy heart, Nancy again prepared the Black Drink and again sent the warnings to her American friends. The Overmountain militias fought the Overhill Cherokee at Boyd's Creek, then withdrew to await reinforcements. While waiting, the American Overmountain men ran out of food. They, too, now wandered the woods in search of dried grapes and hickory nuts.

Nancy hoped that the distressed Americans now might understand the Cherokee's suffering. She rode to "Hungry Camp" and asked Colonel John Sevier to declare a truce. But Sevier refused, saying the Chickamaugas must stop fighting before that was possible. Nancy was disappointed, but still took pity on the starving Americans. She returned to Chota and sent messengers back with some of her remaining cows.

If Nancy hoped her kindness would be rewarded with mercy toward the Overhill towns, that hope was soon dashed. When American reinforcements arrived at deserted Chota, 700 soldiers destroyed the city of sanctuary. On Christmas Eve, the army slaughtered

 Nancy Ward

and ate Nancy's remaining cattle and scoured the woods for the hidden People. The soldiers spent Christmas Day killing twenty-nine men and taking seventeen women and children prisoner. Among the prisoners was Nancy Ward, whom the soldiers escorted to the home of her daughter and son-in-law, Betsy and Joseph Martin.

The backwoods American army established its headquarters in the few Chota dwellings they left standing. Colonel Sevier turned Nancy Ward's home into a command post. Fanning out through the Overhill country, the Americans destroyed several more Overhill towns and burned 50,000 bushels of corn. Joseph Martin knew the suffering this would cause and rode to Chota to protest. When he arrived and discovered that Nancy's cattle had been slaughtered, he jumped off his horse and berated Colonel Elijah Clark for such base treatment of a longtime friend. The two men got into a fistfight, which Colonel Sevier broke up. The commander then begrudgingly agreed to pay Nancy for the cows.

Nancy visited the American officials in Chota several times. Officers slept in her home and filled their bellies with her beef. But Nancy swallowed her grief and anger and begged the American commanders to

The Cherokee Nation

spare the few Overhill towns left standing. The People needed their crops and some refuge other than the forest, Nancy said. But her pleas were ignored, and the remaining Overhill towns were burned to ashes.

Within a year, the Americans had defeated Britain as well as the Cherokee. By 1781, only the Chickamaugas continued to fight with guns provided by the Spanish in Florida. More distressed than ever, the Cherokee obeyed American orders to again "treat for peace" at Long Island. The Cherokee fully expected to have to give up more land in exchange for food, weapons, and the promise of no more attacks on the towns they were trying to rebuild. This time, Nancy was determined to speak. No Cherokee woman had ever spoken before at a treaty council with white men. But Nancy no longer felt compelled to consider white men's ideas about a woman's place. She was the Beloved Woman and she would have her say.

Nancy, now forty-three years old, appealed to the commissioners to acknowledge the common humanity and past friendship of Cherokees and American whites. Dressed in her ceremonial dress and carrying her swans' wing fan, Nancy's black eyes burned with passion as she said: "We are your mothers; you are our sons. Our cry is all for peace; let it continue. This peace

 Nancy Ward

must last forever. Let your women's sons be ours, our sons be yours. Let your women hear our words."

Colonel William Christian answered Nancy:

> Mother, we have listened well to your talk; it is humane. No man can hear it without being moved by it. Such words and thought show the world that human nature is the same everywhere. Our women shall hear your words, and we know how they will feel and think of them. We will not meddle with your People if they will be still and quiet at home and let us live in peace."

The Overhill Cherokee's plight and Nancy's words greatly moved the white Indian agents. Instead of demanding vast new tracts of Cherokee land, they claimed only lands already settled by whites.

Nancy returned to Chota to help rebuild the town, but the city of peace would never regain its past importance. Soon, only the Little Tennessee River separated Chota from white communities. Little Carpenter and Oconostota died of old age. Nancy's married children—and most of the Overhill Cherokee—drifted south and west to where there were fewer white settlers. As the years passed, an endless parade of state and federal officials and private land speculators continued taking more Cherokee lands.

The Cherokee Nation

Not until 1785 did Nancy attend another treaty meeting, and she did so with renewed hope. This time the federal government of an independent America summoned the Cherokee and promised a new age of fair relations with Native Americans. Nancy listened as Indian agents appointed by the Continental Congress said that all previous treaties between colonies, states, and the Cherokee were void. The federal agents also proved the People would be given help to become "civilized." Farm equipment, tools, seed, spinning wheels, looms, gristmills, and other supplies would be donated by the wagon load. The white men's ignorance was showing, for the People had never been uncivilized, Nancy thought. But no longer would the People have to deal with a confusing array of nations, colonies, states, and territories. It sounded as if the land grabs were finally over. Nancy welcomed the promised federal assistance.

When the new Indian agents finished talking, Old Tassel said he hoped the original friendship between red and white people could at last be reestablished. "The red men are the aborigines of this country," Old Tassel said. "It is but a few years since the white men found it. I am of the first stock, a native of this land. The white people are living upon it as our friends.

 Nancy Ward

From the beginning of the friendship between red and white people, beads have been given as confirmation of friendship, as I now give you these beads."

Old Tassel handed the commissioners white beads symbolizing peace, then asked that 3,000 whites living on the Broad and Holston Rivers be removed from Indian land. But the federal agents said that while no more land would be taken, nothing could be done about whites already living on Cherokee land. With no other choice, the Cherokee signed away the occupied land in the Hopewell Treaty. It was the first treaty between the U.S. government and an American Indian tribe, and the Cherokee hoped it would be the last.

As always, Nancy was positive. She stood before the assembled agents and People in her crown of swan feathers and spoke what was in her heart: "I take you by the hand in real friendship . . . I look on you and the red people as my children. Your having determined on peace is most pleasant to me, for I have seen much trouble during the late war. We are now under the protection of Congress and shall have no more disturbances. The talk I have given you is from the young warriors I have raised in my town, as well as myself. They rejoice that we have peace, and hope the chain of friendship will never more be broken."

The Cherokee Nation

Nancy presented the agents with two strings of bright-colored beads, a three-foot white-clay pipe carved with designs and adorned with quills, colorful feathers, and bits of fur. She also presented a pouch of fine West Indian tobacco preferred by the whites.

Later, Nancy's son-in-law, Joseph Martin, protested the Cherokee's concession of already settled lands, but Old Tassel told him to save his breath. "We have held several treaties with the Americans when boundaries were fixed and fair promises made, but we always find that after a treaty they settle much faster than before. Truth is, if we had no land, we should have fewer enemies." Not long after that, a white Indian-hater named Kirk shot Old Tassel while he was standing under a white flag of truce.

Chapter Eight

Granny Ward

After the Hopewell Treaty was signed, Nancy grew more certain that the Cherokee must change to survive and hold onto what land remained. The Cherokee had been overrun and now they faced a rapidly changing world. They must take advantage of the provisions in the Hopewell Treaty that provided material assistance. They must, like the white society, take up large-scale farming and develop cottage industries.

By the 1790s, Bryant Ward had returned to his white family. Nancy left Chota, now a poor village of several houses. She moved sixty-two miles southwest to live with her daughter Betsy Martin, along the Ocee and Hiwassee Rivers. Dragging Canoe had died a few years earlier. The Spanish had settled their border disputes with America, and the Chickamaugas and Americans finally buried the hatchet at Tellico Blockhouse. Peace on the frontier was finally at hand.

The Cherokee Nation

Nancy shared a fine hewn log house in present-day Polk County, Tennessee, with her daughter and grandchildren. Many old friends—white and Cherokee—often visited Nancy in her spacious two-story home. She served them coffee and corncakes. Her guests warmed themselves by her broad stone fireplaces, slept in her wooden beds, drank from her china cups, and admired her spinning wheels and looms. As she aged, people of the area began calling Nancy "Granny Ward." A nearby ford where horse-drawn wagons crossed the river came to be called Granny Ford.

Nancy continued as the Cherokee Beloved Woman and sat on the Cherokee Council. As the years passed, Nancy Ward and the other Cherokee leaders dug in their heels and resisted ongoing state, federal, and private land grabs. But the Cherokee continued losing land. Many white officials resorted to dirty tricks, including bribing and threatening corrupt and demoralized chiefs into signing away land without tribal approval. Nancy opposed the land grabs. But she was careful not to anger federal officials. The Cherokee needed the federal government's continuing gifts and support to thrive. She felt it was unwise to burn those bridges.

Especially important to Cherokee women were

Nancy Ward

government gifts of looms and spinning wheels. Federal officials sent white weavers and spinners to teach Nancy and other older women how to weave and spin wool and cotton. The older women taught the younger women the skills, and soon their cottage industries making wool, cotton, and linen clothing in the style of whites flourished. New Orleans traders bought the yarn, cloth, and clothing that did not sell locally.

Like Nancy, a majority of the Cherokee adopted white ways. Cherokee farms and plantations soon were more lush and productive than those in the surrounding white communities. The Cherokee farmers raised herds of cattle, horses, sheep, and chickens. They grew cotton, tobacco, corn, wheat, oats, potatoes, and the valuable indigo plant that made blue dye for cloth.

A German who came to live among the People built a water-powered grain mill, and Cherokee women began growing and grinding wheat for bread. Two sons of the German mill owner married Nancy's granddaughters. Moravian, Presbyterian, and other Protestant religions started mission schools. Many Cherokee children attended, and some of the People converted

The Cherokee Nation

to Christianity, but not all. Some Cherokees resisted these changes and held fast to their traditional culture. Others mixed and matched white and Cherokee traditions. A couple of thousand Cherokee chose a different path entirely and migrated west where whites were few, game was plentiful, and the People could live as they had before the white man came.

In 1803, a few years after Nancy moved south, the French sold America the western wilderness between the Mississippi River and the Rocky Mountains. Not long after that, the government began pressuring *all* Indians to move to the West. But Nancy and the other Cherokee leaders refused to leave the homeland of their ancestors.

Despite its ongoing efforts to move the tribe west, Nancy remained loyal to the U.S. government. She and the other Cherokee leaders continued to hope that by showing undying loyalty, the whites would finally come to respect the Nation. In 1811, this loyalty led the Cherokee to refuse the invitation of Chief Tecumseh, the great Shawnee leader, to join his tribe and the Creeks in a war to regain their lands. Instead, two years later, 800 Cherokee warriors fought with U.S. General Andrew Jackson against the Shawnee and Creek. Nancy's son Five Killer was among the warriors.

 Nancy Ward

At the close of the Creek War, Nancy welcomed Five Killer home to safety. Soon, the federal government demanded the Cherokee to make more huge land concessions. This was the final straw for Nancy. Not only had warriors died serving the American nation, but the Cherokee people had "civilized" themselves beyond the government's wildest expectations. The new Cherokee capital of Echota had a Council House, court house, printing office, churches, stores, and taverns. The People were developing a U.S.-style government and legal system, a written constitution, a Supreme Court, and a written language. They owned 1,500 slaves, 3,000 plows, 22,000 cattle, 8,000 horses, 760 looms, and 2,500 spinning wheels. They had ten sawmills, thirty-one gristmills, sixty-two blacksmith shops, eight cotton machines, eighteen schools, and eighteen river ferries. Some wealthier families lived in mansions designed by famous architects. From the ashes of defeat, the People had built a thriving and vigorous community. Now the American government wanted to destroy it all.

In 1817, Nancy turned eighty years old. Her hair was as white as cotton wool, and she walked slowly with the help of a carved walking stick. But Nancy Ward walked with a straight back and her coal-black

The Cherokee Nation

eyes shined bright and clear. Although not strong enough to attend the Cherokee Council meetings, she was still the tribe's Beloved Woman. After the Creek War, the Council often debated demands for land concessions and removal to the West. At a critical meeting in 1817, Nancy felt she must strongly oppose both. She sent her son Five Killer to present her walking stick and read a letter. Along with Nancy, twelve leading Cherokee women signed the letter, which read:

> The Cherokee . . . have thought it their duty as mothers to address their beloved chiefs and warriors. We have raised all of you on the land which we now have, which God gave us to inhabit. We do not wish to go to an unknown country. Your mothers, your sisters ask and beg of you not to part with any more of our lands. Keep it for our growing children, for it was the good will of our Creator. Keep your hands off of paper talks. For our children, do not part with any more of our lands, but continue on it and enlarge your farms and cultivate and raise corn and cotton and we, your mothers and sisters, will make clothing for you. It was our desire to forewarn you all not to part with our lands. Warriors take pity and listen to the talk of your sisters . . .

 Nancy Ward

The governing Cherokee Council listened to Nancy's letter, held their debate, and rejected both land concessions and removal.

Not long after that, in the spring of 1822, Nancy Ward died. Her five-year-old great-grandson, Jack Walker Hildebrand, sat by her bedside with her children, grandchildren, and other great-grandchildren. Nancy's white hair spilled across the pillow, and she seemed at peace. As his great-grandmother breathed her last breath, Jack later said, a pale light rose from her body. White like swans down, the light wafted into the air, fluttered in small circles, and grew larger. Then it passed out the open door into the yard. Jack and the others walked to the door to watch as the soft, white light wafted into the sky and grew larger. Slowly the light turned into a white swan, which spread its wings wide and flew northeast over the trees toward Chota, the city of peace and sanctuary.

Afterword

The Trail of Tears

Nancy Ward was buried in an unmarked grave near present-day Benton, Tennessee. Sixteen years after she died, the U.S. Congress passed the Indian Removal Act of 1828. Educated, wealthy, mixed-blood leaders of the Cherokee lobbied the halls of Congress. Senators Daniel Webster and Henry Clay expressed heartfelt opposition. A Supreme Court Decision declared the Removal Act unconstitutional. A good fight was waged which might have turned into war, but then gold was discovered on the remaining Cherokee lands. America's first gold rush spelled doom for the Cherokee. The Cherokee might have won the battle against America for land, but the country's lust for gold was unstoppable.

In 1838, 7,000 American soldiers rounded up 16,000 Cherokee men, women, and children at gunpoint and herded them into corrals. During the cruel, forced

 Nancy Ward

march west known as the *Nunadautsun't*, or Trail of Tears, one-third to half of the captives died.

Not all the Cherokee were herded west. Four hundred North Carolina Cherokee who owned land individually stayed. A thousand more escaped the army by hiding in the hollows of North Carolina's Great Smoky Mountains. The army hunted the escapees, but they had become invisible, like the Nunne'hi.

In 1848, Congress and the state of North Carolina recognized the Eastern Band of Cherokee. Today, more than 8,000 Cherokee live on two reservations in the Great Smoky Mountains. In the West, the removed Cherokee overcame great hardships and entered a golden age of prosperity that lasted until the Civil War. Today more than 90,000 Cherokee live in Oklahoma, and across America there are more than 300,000 Cherokee, making it the largest tribe in the nation.

In 1923, the Chattanooga, Tennessee, Chapter of the Daughters of the American Revolution built a pyramid of quartz fieldstones over Nancy Ward's unmarked grave. Once in a while a stranger visits Nancy's grave and tucks a folded piece of paper in the cracks between the stones. The visitors send personal messages of remembrance and honor to the last Beloved Woman of the Cherokee.

Bibliography

Articles

"The Extention of His Majesty's Dominions: The Virginia Backcountry and the Reconfiguration of Imperial Frontiers." *Journal of American History* 84, no. 4 (1998): 1281-1312.

King, Duane H. "Long Island of the Holston: Sacred Cherokee Ground." *Journal of Cherokee Studies* 1 (1976): 113-127.

Lillard, Roy G. "The Story of Nancy Ward, 1738-1822." *Daughters of the American Revolution Magazine* 110, no. 1 (1976): 42-43, 158.

"Manufactured History: Refighting the Battle of Point Pleasant," *West Virginia History* 56 (1997): 76-87.

Norman, Geoffrey. "Two Nations, One People—The Cherokee." *National Geographic* 187, no. 1 (May 1995): 72-97.

Shirk, Willis L., Jr. "The 'Scots-Irish' of Donegal Township, 1716-1815." *Journal of the Lancaster County Historical Society* 101, no. 1 (1999): 8-35.

Nancy Ward

Symonds, Craig. "The Failure of America's Indian Policy on the Southwestern Frontier, 1785-1793." *Tennessee Historical Quarterly* 35, no. 1 (1976): 29-45.

Tucker, Norma. "Nancy Ward, Ghigha of the Cherokees." *Georgia Historical Quarterly* 53, no. 2 (1969): 192-200.

"Tennessee Indian History: Creativity and Power," *Tennessee Historical Quarterly* 54, no. 4 (1995): 286-305.

Williams, David. "Gold Fever: The Cherokee Nation and the Closing of Georgia's Frontier." *Proceedings and Papers of the Georgia Association of Historians* 11 (1990): 24-29.

Books

Adair, James. *History of the American Indians*. Samuel Cole Williams, ed. Johnson City, TN: The Watauga Press, 1930.

Allen, Paula Gunn. *As Long As the Rivers Flow: The Stories of Nine Native Americans*. New York: Scholastic Trade, 1996.

———. *The Sacred Hoop*. Boston: Beacon Press, 1992.

Anderson, William L., ed. *Cherokee Removal, Before and After*. Athens, Georgia: Univ. of GA Press, 1991.

Bataille, Gretchen, and Kathleen Sands. *American Indian Women: A Research Guide*. Garland Publishing, 1991.

Berkin, Carol, and Leslie Horowitz, eds. *Women's Voices, Women's Lives: Documents in Early American History*. Chicago: Northeastern Univ. Press, 1998.

Berkin, Carol. *First Generations: Women in Colonial America*. New York: Hill and Wang, 1996.

The Cherokee Nation

Burns, Annie Walker. *Ward families history records of the Eastern Cherokee tribe.* Washington, D.C.: The National Archives, (Room 5-W) [19?].

Calloway, Brenda C. *America's First Western Frontier: East Tennessee: A Story of the Early Settlers and Indians of East Tennessee.* Johnson City, TN: Overmountain Press, 1989.

Chapman, Jefferson. *Tellico Archaeology: 12,000 Years of Native American History*, Revised Edition. Knoxville: The Univ. of TN Press, 1995.

Davis, Donald Edward. "Where There Be Mountains: Environmental and Cultural Change in the Appalachian South, 1500-1800." (abstract in Dissertation Abstracts International 55 (1994): 758A.

Demos, John. *The Tried and the True: Native American Women Confronting Colonization* (Young Oxford History of Women in the United States, Vol. 1). London: Oxford Univ. Press, 1998.

Duane Champagne, ed. *Native America: Portrait of the Peoples.* Detroit: Visible Ink Press, 1994, pp. 567-593.

Eckert, Allan W. *The Frontiersmen, A Narrative.* Boston: Little, Brown, 1967.

Ellington, Charlotte Jane. *Beloved Mother: The Story of Nancy Ward.* Johnson City, TN: The Overmountain Press, 1994.

Finger, John R. *The Eastern Band of Cherokees, 1819-1900.* Knoxville: The Univ. of TN Press, 1984.

Foster, J Michael K., Jack Campisi and Marianne Mithun, eds. *Extending the Rafters: Interdisciplinary Approaches to Iroquois Studies.* Albany: SUNY Press, 1984.

Nancy Ward

Galloway, Colin, G. *New Worlds for All: Indians, Europeans, and the Remaking of Early America*. Baltimore: Johns Hopkins Univ. Press, 1997.

Green, Rayna. *Women in American Indian Society*. Broomall, PA: Chelsea House, 1992.

Hatley, Thomas M. *The Dividing Paths: Cherokees and South Carolinians Through the Era of Revolution*. New York: Oxford Univ. Press, 1993.

Hudson, Charles. *The Southeastern Indians*. Knoxville: The Univ. of TN Press, 1976.

King, Duane, ed. *The Cherokee Indian Nation: A Troubled History*. Knoxville: The Univ. of TN Press, 1979.

Lewis, Thomas M. N., and Madeline Kneberg. *Tribes that Slumber*. Knoxville: The Univ. of TN Press, 1958.

McWhorter, Lucullus Virgil. *The Border Settlers of Northwestern Virginia from 1768 to 1795; Embracing the Life of Jesse Hughes, and Other Noted Scouts of the Great Woods of the Trans-Alleghency*. Richwood, WV: Jim Comstock Pub, 1973.

Metcalfe, Samuel Lytler. *A Collection of Some of the Most Interesting Narratives of Indian Warfare in the West Wilkinson, St. Clair & Wayne: The Whole Compiled from the Best Authorities*. New York: W. Abbatt, 1913.

Moody, James. *Myths of the Cherokee*. New York: Johnson Reprint Corp., 1970.

Niethammer, Carolyn. *Daughters of the Earth: The Lives and Legends of American Indian Women*. New York: Collier, 1977.

Norton, Mary Beth. *Founding Mothers & Fathers: Gendered Power and the Forming of American Society*. New York: A.A. Knopf, 1996.

The Cherokee Nation

———.*Liberty's Daughters: The Revolutionary Experience of American Women, 1750-1800*. Boston: Little, Brown, 1980.

Paredes, J. Anthony, ed. *Indians of the Southeastern United States in the Late 20th Century*. Tuscaloosa, AL: The Univ. of AL Press, 1992.

Perdue, Theda, *Cherokee Women: Gender and Culture Change, 1700-1835*. Lincoln: Univ. of NE Press, 1998.

Reid, John Phillip. *A Better Kind of Hatchet: Law, Trade, and Diplomacy in the Cherokee Nation During the Early Years of European Contact*. University Park: PA State Univ. Press, 1976.

Rights, Douglas L., *The American Indian in North Carolina*. Durham, NC: Duke Univ. Press, 1947.

Salmon, Marylynn. *The Limits of Independence: American Women, 1760-1800* (The Young Oxford History of Women in the United States, Vol. 3). London: Oxford Univ. Press, 1994.

Shoemaker, Nancy. *Negotiators of Change: Historical Perspectives on Native American Women*. New York: Routledge, 1995.

Sturtevant, William C, ed. *Handbook of North American Indians*. Washington, D.C.: Smithsonian Institution, 1978.

Usner, Daniel H. *Indians, Settlers & Slaves in a Frontier Exchange Economy: The Lower Mississippi Valley Before 1783*. Chapel Hill: Univ. of NC Press, 1992.

Van Every, Dale. *Forth to the Wilderness; The First American Frontier, 1754-1774*. New York, Morrow, 1961.

Williams, Samuel. *Early Travels in the Tennessee Country, 1540-1800*. Johnson City, TN: The Watauga Press, 1928.

Index

American Civil War, 104
American Revolution, 86
Anne, Queen of England, 24
Attakullakulla, Peace Chief of Chota (Little Carpenter), 15, 18-26, 28, 31-32, 45, 47, 53-54, 56-57, 65, 68, 76, 81-82, 92

Badger, 22
Battle of Taliwa, 41-42, 44
Brown, Jacob, 64

Cameron, Alexander, 65
Chota, 9-13, 15-16, 18-22, 24, 29, 31-32, 34, 37, 39, 42-44, 48, 50-51, 53, 57, 67-68, 71, 73, 76, 78-81, 89-90, 92, 96, 102

Christian, William, 81-82, 85, 92
Clark, Elijah, 90
Clay, Henry, 103
Continental Congress, 93
Cornstalk, Chief, 73-76
Cornwallis, British General, 88
Cuming, Alexander, 23

Declaration of Independence, 85
Dinwiddie, Royal Governor of Virginia, 53
Doublehead, 76
Dragging Canoe, War Chief of Great Island Town, 22, 50-51, 53, 56, 68-72, 74, 76-77, 79, 81-82, 96

The Cherokee Nation

Echota, 100

Five Killer (father), 21
Five Killer (son), 34, 100-101
Forbes, John, 50
Fort Caswell, 78
Fort Dobbs, 48
Fort Duquesne, 50
Fort Loudoun, 48, 50, 57-58
Fort Prince George, 48, 55-56, 59
Fox, 23
French and Indian War, 47, 62, 64

George II, King of England, 23-25, 32
George III, King of England, 61, 73
Grant, James, 60
Great Smoky Mountains, 104
Green Corn Festival, 10, 14-16

Henderson, Richard, 67, 69-70
Hildebrand, Jack Walker, 102
Hopewell Treaty, 94, 96

Indian Removal Act of 1828, 103

Jackson, Andrew, 99
Jefferson, Thomas, 88

Ka-ti (daughter), 34, 36
Kingfisher (husband), 33-36, 39-41, 45

Lantagnac, Ambassador, 52
Little Owl, 22
Long Fellow (brother), 10, 15, 22
Long Island Treaty, 85
Lyttleton, Royal Governor of South Carolina, 54-56

Martin, Betsy (Ward), 46, 86, 90, 96
Martin, Joseph, 85-86, 90, 95

Oconostota, War Chief of Chota, 18, 20, 22-23, 25, 38, 44, 53-57, 68, 70, 82, 92
Old Tassel, Peace Chief of Chota, 82-84, 93-95
Old Weasel, 13-14, 20

 Nancy Ward

Pitt, William, 50

Raven, Chief of Chota, 19-20, 39, 41, 69, 76

Saloue, Chief, 52
Sevier, John, 81-82, 89-90
Standing Turkey, 38
Star, Caleb, 81
Stuart, John, 61

Tame Doe (mother), 9, 11, 13, 15, 18, 21, 27-28, 31, 33, 36, 43-44
Tecumseh, Chief, 99
Thomas, Isaac, 77
Trail of Tears, 104
Transylvania Land Company, 67

Ward, Bryant, 45-47, 57, 64, 77, 86, 88, 96
Ward, Nancy, Beloved Woman of the Cherokee (Nanye-hi),
  aiding settlers, 48, 50, 57-58, 64, 77-80
  at Battle of Taliwa, 36-41
  childhood, 9-16, 18-27, 30-32

death, 102
education, 28-29, 35-36
marriages, 33-34, 45-46
named Beloved Woman, 43-45
old age, 96-101
as peace delegate, 53-56, 91-95
Wauhatchie, Chief, 52
Webster, Daniel, 103
Willenawah, (uncle), 57-58

Young Tassel, 76